UNPACKED

AN OLD SOUL'S GUIDE TO THE ART OF
RELOCATION

CHRISTINE KRAFT

CONTENTS

"Christine is a talented soul, and her steady, calming voice, amidst what is inevitable relocation chaos, is charming. She has a fantastic way of 'unpacking' so many emotional challenges of moving yet putting them into a wonderfully spirited perspective that is incredibly relatable and soothing to the reader. I think all of us have a relocation story of some sort in our past that will be touched by her gentle and illustrative words and examples. As a clinical psychologist, I think everyone should 'unpack' their issues – it will make them feel better. I recommend this to anyone who has had to move, period. This book is good therapy!"

— LISA HOROWITZ, PHD, CLINICAL PSYCHOLOGIST, BETHESDA, MARYLAND

"Relocating is hard, and Christine Kraft is just the wise, been-there guide you need to walk you through a bout of dislocation fever. She's open, calming, and centering, and her counsel will help you see the messy before, during, and after of your move as a sacred narrative of growth. With *Unpacked*'s simple exercises and explanations, even the most jaded relocation artist will find a way to make a home wherever they are."

— MELODY WARNICK, AUTHOR OF *THIS IS WHERE YOU BELONG: FINDING HOME WHEREVER YOU ARE*

This humble guide is dedicated to Yasuyo and courageous relocation artists making moves all over the world. Let's find each other and make the world a better place.

To be a soulful person means to go against all the pervasive, prove-yourself values of our culture and instead treasure what is unique and internal and valuable in yourself and your own personal evolution.

— DR. JEAN SHINODA BOLEN

FOREWORD

What a delightful, fresh topic Christine Kraft has chosen to write about! Little did she know when she asked me to write the foreword, that I am the child of a traveling father; our family loyally trooped along with him as his career as a trouble-shooting manage-ment consultant unfolded – from the East Coast to the West Coast and back to the East Coast, then west across the country in increments. I went to three different high schools, lived in wealthy suburbs of large cities and on farms with cows, sheep, and horses. I even went to one of the last one-room country schools during our couple years outside Kansas City.

I know quite well the stages of packing and unpacking, saying goodbye and hello, and over-coming shyness to find a new sense of belonging. We don't usually think of moving as a spiritual experience, but I credit the diversity of my upbringing for my ability to relate to anyone, to feel the quality of energy in different places, and to value the power of surprise and fluidity. So, though moving so many times – at least twenty for our family – presented many challenges, it also created great open-mindedness and creativity in all of us.

Christine has done a deep dive into all the subtle aspects of relocation, touching on the physical aspects of this sort of change and, interestingly, relating each mundane phase to the personal process of growth and evolution we all go through in life. She has created a roadmap for you for each of the phases, with things to pay attention to, techniques for easing through the stuck points, and intuitive insights about positive ways of perceiving the difficult or unknown parts.

This book will certainly help you find the gifts in this sort of major life change. Even when a new place doesn't totally resonate with you, you can find its beauty and focus on something to nourish your soul. The world is an amazingly diverse, lush, complicated, stimulating, and peace-generating place, especially when you tune in to the land beneath your feet and to the kind of flora and fauna living there with you. Every new thing in your environment – the weather, the layout of the town, the consciousness of the locals – matches something inside you that you may not have realized was part of you, or that you needed to activate in yourself.

Relocating may bring up painful emotions, but you will soon see that both the people and place you are leaving, and the people and place you are discovering are inextricable parts of you. You never lose the experiences. Not to sound too far out but you learn that you are part of a large energetic grid of interconnected lines and nodes and that network of experiences eventually becomes your personal "energy body," if you will. All the lines of connection, all the relationships with people, land, and ecosystems – the whole thing sources you.

Christine writes well. I like the stories she uses to demonstrate the points she makes. They give the book the personal touch and make it human. And, her own experiences help us more easily integrate the inner work involved in each of the three phases of this "rite of passage." She reminds us that relocating is a lesson in spiritual mobility and "place-making," not just physical movement.

Christine says, "One of the most exciting things about moving a lot is looking back and admiring the mover's mindset you've earned for yourself. With your tuned-up mover's mindset, I bet you start seeing yourself as a powerhouse, not simply as a trailing spouse or a moving mouse, timid and hiding from life. Step into your power and place, and see what kind of difference you can make right where you've landed." To me, this is the essence of the spiritual path – learning to embrace fluidity and yet be in the moment with full presence, engaging with reality as it arises, without judgment or projection of possible repercussions or outcomes.

This is a jewel of a book, about a topic not too many people have addressed well. It certainly validates all my experience of moving on – from early childhood through teenage years to adulthood. You learn something important at any age by letting go and recreating your reality.

Penney Peirce
Author of *Transparency, Frequency, Leap of Perception,*
and *The Intuitive Way*
Ormond Beach, FL
October 2020

MOVING AGAIN?

I wrote this book for you – a talented soul who is planning to accompany a spouse on another big relocation. You have done this several times already and are surprised that, at this point in life, while friends are downsizing and traveling, making new relationships and careers, you are relocating...again.

I know you well.

You are hardworking, creative, and dynamic. You are smart, and, more than that, you are experienced. You are an expert mover, confident that you will be able to manage all of the relocation details and will put your spouse and family in front of you as you have done a dozen times before.

You are flexible, adaptable, and generous. A long time ago, you had a dream that you would live adventurously and romantically, you would marry young, and you and your spouse would grow old together. If you ever had children, they would be raised to be modern and to seek a global perspective. When you looked back, you hoped to feel pride, a sense that you were making a unique mark on the world with your family lifestyle.

Your vision of the good life would be worth the trade-offs implied. Much more than financial prosperity, your good life was about cultivating in yourself and your family an appreciation for differences in culture, ethnicity, geography, politics, food, art, history, and tradition. You wanted to maintain a bright spirit, friends from all walks of life, and simple routines that comforted you while forging deep relationships with lifelong friends along well-traveled common ground.

Guess what? You did it, at least for a bit.

And then you moved and did it again. Perhaps even again and again.

Through it all, you evolved, and your life became a work of art in progress. With each move, with each trade-off, you felt yourself drifting farther from "home" as personal, professional, and family goals changed.

The losses and the joys were part of the deal, you reasoned, so with each move your brilliant spouse proposed, you lived the life of yes, and onward you went.

On balance, you have been extremely lucky and

privileged. You give thanks for all you have, and you understand your struggles are nothing compared to the challenges facing the unhoused. Since you are humble, you don't dare call any attention to your gripes, at least not until now.

You have made creating a beautiful home wherever you are look easy. You have cultivated a servant's heart, and you've likely even thrived in a variety of roles and locations.

Why are you finding yourself so surprised by the emotionality you feel about this upcoming move?

Something is changing, but it isn't clear what. When your friends joke that it is hormones, there is probably some truth to their chiding. And yet, you wonder if there isn't something else going on. Perhaps you feel like this move is causing you to examine your life to date in a way that feels like there is a particular urgency to "get it right, finally."

You haven't been sleeping well, and you have withdrawn from your friends, even though you know you don't have much time together before you move again.

When thoughts surface that you have become much too dependent on your partner, you feel trapped and even a bit panicked. It feels so forbidden to touch the fear and the anger you sense building up, but what are your options?

You were just starting to settle down and think about getting back to projects long abandoned, and now another move? It's a bit too much, and that's when you feel that flash of fear that maybe you'll break this time.

The worst thing is that you are ashamed of these feelings. You love your spouse and support their success unequivocally, but what you want is that someplace like home feeling you have always imagined. That is what you have been working for.

You want to stay where you are and dig in. You want to stop the back-and-forth of having to reinvent everything about your identity while holding onto a marriage that you worry has grown incredibly out of date. You are tired of all the change.

When will it be your time to get back to dreams on hold, you wonder?

But wait, haven't many of your dreams already come true?

You've lived in some amazing places and have experienced so many of the world's riches, even in challenging times, while raising children and working to adjust to many levels of change.

Perhaps that is the hardest part, to realize that while your life is so rich and many of your dreams have come true, you are still yearning for an unfolding of something intangible. It seems within reach if only you could settle down and stop moving around so much.

As the children launch toward their individual goals – college, jobs, and communities filled with their future loves – you sense that the promise of the middle years could be fun. How can you admit that you are angry and resentful about the timing of this move when you have so many blessings?

You stay silent and try to make the best of it.

Joking and keeping busy, you maintain a head-down stance until something clicks, and you start asking why? Why should you even go with him this time?

Why is moving this time so different? What happened to my energy?

Perhaps you buried your mom last year, and all you can do is think about how you wish you could get on the phone with her and have a cry. Perhaps she'd encourage you to let him move on his own while you stay back and relish the continuity your soul is craving. Is there anyone else that understands this dilemma?

When you talk to your husband, he thinks you staying back with the boys is a terrible idea. He says he will miss you madly and asks you to please come with him. When you say you are worried to move the kids again, he says they are fine, nearly all grown up, so they'll be okay. We'll get them all the therapy they need, he assures you.

A disconnect fills the room, and you realize that your options are stark: you either go for it and accompany your spouse on the next move, or you end your marriage.

Unwilling to leave the marriage after twenty-eight years (and the love, comforts, family, and financial success you've built together), you decide your problem is that you just have the blues. Ah, the blues.

Perhaps your good life, you are ashamed to admit, is contributing to you feeling invisible and isolated, but since you have been complicit in the moving lifestyle for decades, you can't see a way out now.

Until you have another option, you are going to accompany your spouse, and you will just have to find a way to settle down and shift into a creative, meaningful rhythm that helps you get your groove back. That's it, you think. I'll just have to clarify who I am and what is important to me in my next new town.

You feel a flash of relief. You've got this. And that's when the ten canvasses still crated from your last move come to mind, and you renew your plan to finish them as soon as you touch down and get settled in the next place.

You make a promise to put yourself at the top of your to-do list when you next land. But then the phone rings, and you get sidetracked, and just like that, you are online to search housing, purchase moving supplies, and check out local reviews guiding you to the best schools, doctors, and dry cleaners; the list goes on and on.

Sound familiar? I get it, and it is the nature of relocation. It is not a straight line; it is a process that takes its time.

If there were a magic potion I could make to expedite your feeling of ease in this upcoming move, I would. Instead, I am writing you a book so that you have a gentle reminder whenever you need it that the timeframe for adjusting to a move is never in your hands.

The timeframe for a move is an unfolding of your particular soul at a particular time, place, geography, and moment in history. Trust that this moment, the particularities of the present moment before you, including the geography of your next destination, holds everything you need for your precious soul's unfolding.

In this book, you'll learn that it is not necessary to struggle with your upcoming move. The choice to live boldly awaits, in spite of all the change ahead. The call to move forward awaits, even if you are uncertain about whether now is the right time to move – with a spouse, your pets, your children, your parents, your friends, or for love itself. In spite of what we know will be goodbyes, farewells, "I'm sorrys," and "I love yous," now is the time.

The choice to center in this moment is an incon-venient act of courage and one that just might save you from extended discouragement and disorientation after the move. I see you, and I believe in you. In fact, I was you.

If you can commit to showing up in this moment of your move, with all of its reminders of your impermanence – you can learn to recognize and be comforted by the awareness that, in spite of all the changes and the emotions, you are still here, still present and as beautiful as a river, changing every day.

You will become a mindful mover, conscious that you are both the particle of water and the wave moving it.

Let's begin.

2

MY STORY

You might wonder what makes me qualified to write an entire book about the accompanying spouse's wild journey to becoming a mindful mover. I am seeking to give voice to an aspect of my life that I feel I have concealed on some level, but, even more so, I am writing to help other relocation experts like me walk the fine line between the heartbreak and privilege many of us know so well, but find increasingly difficult to talk about.

Up until the global pandemic put me on pause, I was a closeted accompanying spouse. The old-fashioned term "trailing spouse" was not how I saw myself. I considered myself a team player. After all, the role chose me, not the other way around, and I managed to keep a career simmering on the back-burner in spite of lots of competing roles.

But I started using the term "accompanying

spouse" when I moved to California in my fifties because it felt different from prior moves. At fifty, I was no longer as consumed by my role as Brooks' wife and mother to our two children. I had grown more interested in getting back to doing my own thing.

I had juggled moving my career, house, and kids with joy and energy at earlier stages, but with the seasons shifting, the urgency to solidify my tribe and settle into one or two of my life's other big callings in my middle years was palpable. It was in this last move that I became an accompanying spouse and started to touch the powerful feelings of conflict that had me questioning everything.

MOVING INWARD

I felt resentful that after so many decades of devoted parenting and spousing, after so much dismantling – dismantling of homes, gardens, friendships, and dreams in development – I didn't have more to show for it. While we had managed to put dollars in the bank account, in terms of self-expression or concrete contributions to my professional creative interests – things I valued mightily – I had little to show.

I lacked a sense of a legacy beyond the children and the house and garden, and I judged myself for it. It's even difficult to write that out now, here.

The truth is that I was unprepared to manage

these uncomfortable feelings when they stirred in me because they left me feeling diminished; they challenged my core sense of self as someone who could manage. Because Brooks' career in the news business involved his nearly constant travel on an unpredictable schedule across time zones, I found it hard to carve out adequate stability to fully focus on my career.

That meant my career achievements frequently shape-shifted and, in time, grew diffuse in order to adapt. Brooks' career success, on the other hand, followed a straighter line along an upward trajectory to phenomenal success (I cover more about this dynamic later in the book).

Woefully unprepared to manage professional trade-offs while raising kids, I was also unprepared to manage the fallout our moves caused in my sensitive inner life. I naively assumed I could do it all, which meant I didn't have the language to frame the conflict I felt inside in a way that honored both the marriage and my emerging sense of self as a talented working mother who worried she was losing an opportunity to pursue her own professional goals.

There never seemed to be enough time or the right time to dig in and work through what felt like a deep sense of abandonment of my dreams. I also had difficulty not feeling abandoned by my husband, whose work in faraway, exotic places drew a stark contrast to the more basic daily toil of raising children while making adjustments to a new town. The patriarchal value of career outside of the home was a strong unexamined theme in my life during these years.

Therapy was a flop, as I experienced tremendous gender bias; in my opinion, conventional couple's therapy is good at upholding traditional social roles and the status quo, something I was already doing out of a personal sense of obligation and devotion to my marriage and family. What I needed was support mapping the other side of the story, the mortal limits of a wife and mother, and the support for putting language on the intangible trade-offs I was encountering in my moves.

What I needed was a way to look at the challenges of our situation from a much higher plane, as the eagle flies, so to speak.

Looking back, I longed for a more spiritual understanding of my partnership with my husband, and I also longed for a more soulful acceptance of my humble path, but I felt conflicted about the choices I seemed to be making or that the world was making for me.

These sentiments were all mixed up with nowhere to go, so I just kept trying to carry on with an open heart. I was a single parent much of the time, but I did not have to pay for all of our expenses, which was a blessing. Thankfully, I read a lot and loved walking in nature, so I started turning to meditation and nature walks as a path to inner peace and acceptance.

Because moving challenged my life plans, it forced me to modify many long-term goals. I had to simplify and become less materialistic, nimbler, and much more creative – not a bad transformation for a soul when written out so matter-of-factly. You might say that I became a minimalist by moving a lot, and while it hurt like hell, the result has a kind of clarity and luminance that is organic and healing.

Now I enjoy supporting others on the winding path to becoming a relocation artist. Whether moving for a job, for a sad season, for an adventure, or just to downsize into the later years, moving will change a person from the inside out. Further, it may challenge a person to the core, which is why some resist moving, delaying the changes that they know inside would be healthy for them.

THE HUMBLE TEACHER

Moving has been a humble teacher. It has taught me that the most reliable way to feel at home in the world is to create a rich inner life through contact and connection with everyday nature, as opposed to experiencing nature at its peak. Seeking nature at its peak can be expensive and can also be an ego trip. It isn't my jam because I was drawn to a path of deepening my acceptance of what was since I felt so deeply obligated to keep showing up in it. In other words, I didn't seek an "away" frame as much as I did a frame that helped me accept myself and my life just as it was.

Everyday nature is the most generous teacher because she takes you just as you are and inspires you to become something more. She teaches you about the seasons, about the necessity of a fallow field, about the abundance of the harvest, and about the ancient rhythms of the moon, the tide, the patterns. She's medicine, really.

By surrendering again and again to what hurt and what helped me in various new settings, nature's persistent presence taught me to be a better friend to myself by abandoning the deadly narrative of self-judgment and limitation, fueled by old systems of limited human thinking. She taught me to cease judgment of the wild variety of legitimate life on this planet and to learn to love a bigger version of the world and a more humble version of myself, wherever I was planted. She taught me to keep showing up, even if that meant learning how to be alone long enough to map the difference between being alone and feeling lonely.

While I have had to say goodbye to people and places I've loved, and to dreams and ambitions interrupted, moving has taught me not to say goodbye to myself. Cliché as it sounds, I'm a better soul for the trade-offs moving put in play for me. Cultivating a rich inner life, one home at a time, in one city at a time, may be just enough of a legacy to satisfy this old soul's earthly drives. That's why I'm sharing what I know with you.

GRATITUDE FOR THE MOVING LIFE

I have spent years keeping receipts on the pros, cons, and in-betweens of relocating for a spouse's job. I have been an upbeat, place-making housewife who is smart, caring, and hardworking, and I have been a sad, lost soul who envies her hubby's success because she hoped she'd be a star too and didn't know there was another path with merit calling her forth.

While I never set out for the moving life, it is the life I have lived. My moving mindset is about not forcing the adjustment and, instead, giving myself a lot of room to find my way. This allows me to stay open enough to handle whatever complexities and polarities moving exposes.

In spite of my gratitude for all the opportunities moving has brought, it is also true that I now live with what I call a low-grade dislocation fever. I don't expect it to go away, and I treat it with a deepening relationship to nature, birds, and trees in particular.

After residing in eleven homes in twenty-five years and leaving so many people, places, and things

I love, one might say that moving has forged me into a citizen of the world.

WHAT IS HOME ANYWAY?

I grew up in a small town on the east end of Long Island. We were surrounded by open space, majestic wetlands, quaint whaling villages, and Indigenous territories colonized by the English in the 1600s. My big dream was to be an actress and comedienne, helping people laugh and heal. In time I dropped the acting part, honed my sense of humor and love for people, and accepted any and every role life handed me on my path to become a healer.

Cupid's arrow struck me at twenty-one years old with a love for Brooks Kraft, a budding photojournalist raised in New York City with roots on the North Fork of Long Island. I figured we'd evolve into an NYC-LI couple at some point. It would happen; I was certain because the only blueprint for life I had seen up close at twenty-one was to work in NYC and spend all weekend in nature on Long Island.

When I went to college and people would say, "I know the Hamptons," I would be startled. To me, my hometown of three square miles was singular, not part of a branded vacation region. As a townie from the east end of Long Island, I could describe in detail the multitude of differences between my hamlet and another just a couple miles down the road. "No two wetlands are alike, and have you noticed how the wind moves along the bay?" I would whisper to anyone who would listen.

Perhaps this is why I have always yearned to return to the particular comforts one's deep knowledge of a single place provides. That deep knowing itself is home to me; it is something I hold in my heart and senses. For now, though, adapting to new habitats has been my path to someplace like home.

THE BOSTON YEARS

When Brooks and I married, we were living in our first home in Cambridge, Massachusetts, near Harvard Square. I attended graduate school and, within months, he was traveling with Nelson Mandela, covering the first free election in South Africa. He returned from that assignment with his first magazine covers and shrapnel in his back from stray bullets fired by protesters along the campaign trail.

During those Boston years, we had both of our beloved children, and we bought and sold three homes. The last move was short-lived but long grieved by me. It was a beautiful, 1890s Victorian with three old fireplaces and lots of detail. It was my forever house, a money pit too, but I dreamed that in time we'd fill its old rooms and wrap around porch with friends and family and good times for decades to come. That dream was cut short.

Just eighteen months after moving into the forever house, Brooks got his big break in photojournalism. He was offered a juicy position to cover the White House for *Time* magazine. This was just six months after 9/11. While most people were frightful that further acts of terror were likely, we shuttered our beautiful Victorian, packed up our toddlers, and said goodbye to twelve years of friendships, memories, and geography we loved. We moved right inside the Beltway into what felt like a danger zone. I wondered if I had lost my mind.

On moving day, I sobbed so primally that I frightened my friend, Eliza. She and I would run and hike together, and I loved being a new mother with her wise friendship by my side. What would I do without such a friend, someone who saw me evolving from a young twenty-something into a mother of two, and someone who overlooked my shortcomings and built up my strengths?

THE MOVE TO WASHINGTON

I don't remember much about the transition from Boston to D.C., except that I white-knuckled it. I thought, just push on. Go forward, and all will be okay. You have to. You have two kids, and you'll figure out how to adjust. The adjustment took forever, probably because I was also learning how to raise school-age children and reestablish my career; I was flying the plane while building it too.

While the children were young, the pressure to fit in and conform felt immense to me. There was a constant physical and emotional need to tend to. I carried on through all of those moments, and I did my best to impart core values, understanding, and a love for the world as it is, even as I struggled through many very difficult parenting years, which I won't cover in this book.

Washington, D.C., is unlike any city in America. It is a small town in many respects, with the sophistication of a world-class global city. I found the mighty Potomac so mysterious; it wound through the city, whispering history itself. It was the deadliest body of water I've ever learned to read, and while I missed my Atlantic shores, I ultimately fell in love with the river and my birdwatching adventures along the C&O Canal.

I'll spare you how I struggled with the humidity, the constant air patrols, the choppers, the sniper, the horrendous traffic, and the mind-numbing politics, and instead share that it was through a series of losses in D.C. that I was pushed into a deeper relationship with nature. It was there I honed my intuitive abilities and worked with birds and trees, enjoying all manner of quiet hikes and paddles along the Potomac with extraordinary friends in extraordinary nature.

It took me about eight to ten years to adjust because I was still hung up on thinking there was a "right place for me" somewhere and that I wouldn't have such struggles if I could just figure out where that place was.

With responsibility for the children starting to ease and my friendships and community ties truly deepening after fifteen years, I had just started to deeply attach to the place when Brooks received another highly sought-after opportunity to work on a small team at Apple as a photographer helping develop their visual story. I was thrilled for him, and I was pretty convinced I wasn't going to accompany him. We had a daughter heading to college, and our son was just a sophomore in high school.

RELOCATING AT FIFTY

I was happy for Brooks. He had been running his freelance business for twenty years and was successful in spite of many challenges. While I had worked as the lead developer of personal health stories over the years and had created glimmering moments of career success, I found the constraints of Brooks' frequent and often unplanned travel highly impactful on the kids and me. I curbed my career aspirations in part to accommodate his professional reality because he was, after all, the steady earner. He dislikes it when I make that kind of statement so succinctly, and, admittedly, we still have work to do to create a shared narrative about how his career impacted mine. (Most couples have a version of that story, but perhaps ours is more pronounced given his choice of career and my adaptability, but I digress.)

The way I see it, someone had to pick up the slack and stay present, even if we had some hired help. While he was (and is) a great father who helped out with chores, care, and laundry, I was the parent who steadfastly covered home base for the team and curbed my individual goals.

After a ninety-day period of contemplation of various scenarios around the move to California, we agreed that it was better for us all to stick together. The distance between coasts was not for a commuter marriage, and, as our son got his learner's permit and started to shoot up in height, the thought of separating him from daily contact with his father seemed ill-timed. I agreed to accompany the family on the move for two to three years and then would reassess.

DISMANTLING AGAIN

Brooks began his new position out West just weeks after the offer came. That left me to organize the house and all the affairs and to single-handedly shepherd our teenagers through the remainder of the school year. It was December, and we would move in mid-June. It was a huge job and one I underestimated.

We had been in our house for fifteen years, and it was a big house by my standards. It also held many wonderful memories, so the inner work of moving was a heavy lift.

Since we didn't know where we would live in California, and I am against paying to store furniture when so many families need it urgently, we donated more than eight rooms of usable furniture. We kept our dishes, pots, pans, portable appliances, as well as a few antiques, most of our books, Brooks' archives, and a bunch of art.

When moving day came, we flew – with the kids (seventeen and nineteen) and our two rescue dogs – out to sunny California and moved into a rental house in the foothills of the Santa Cruz Mountains. That began our transition, and, as we felt our way through the relocation Marco Polo game, we enjoyed the early memories of the West Coast, including a rental house with a pool, just like the movies we envisioned.

But like all relocations, there is an adjustment to expectations. In time, it became clear that our expensive Silicon Valley rental house would require me to serve as its nearly full time (unpaid) house manager. As the California sun blazed down on us, I experienced my first hot flash on a day that was 107 degrees. We were told the house didn't need air conditioning.

Somehow we caught our breath, launched our daughter to college, got our son started at a new high school, when, just as Brooks' travel schedule swelled up again, my father passed away. Nothing prepared me for the unmoored feelings his death gave way to within.

As grief enveloped me, I was lost, and I hated myself for following my husband in this first year. I resented the instant life he had at work, and I resented the extent to which I was expected to reinvent myself and our social support system on my own. Plus, I didn't much care for the tech narratives about the good life that were fed to me from our overpriced rental.

The good life to me was an integrated adventure that included a strong moral compass; great books; a mindset of abundance; a sense of virtue, service, connectedness; and a sense of engagement with community. Prosperity without all of those other things was not prosperity; it was vanity, no?

Had I become a demanding wife?

The root cause of my demands was not so much constant dissatisfaction as much as it was fear, grief, and a sense of defeat. I realize that nuance is lost in the midst of marital conflicts, and our arguments took on a polarized quality that lacked all nuance.

Most therapists cannot untangle this kind of yarn knot, which surfaces again and again as a power struggle, without investing a great deal of time with the couple to support the partners shared commitment to doing the work of revising.

It was then that Brooks and I started bickering about everything. We bickered about all of the small things and all of the big things too. As our son approached his launch to college, my confidence in my ability to stay with the family in California faltered dramatically.

With high standards and a lonely marriage, I drank too much and did it alone. I ate too much and did that alone too. I fell into grief and looked backward, not forward. On top of it, I had a hard time finding a hairdresser.

The hair thing sounds silly, but don't underestimate the rogue self-doubt that a hair crisis can contribute to a relocation crisis. After I paid way too much for a cut and color that made me look like I was wearing a wig, I decided to let my hair come in naturally. Since I didn't know who I was, I shouldn't try to keep myself looking like someone I used to be. At least that was my reasoning.

The good stuff started for me when I recommitted to staying with Brooks and my decision to relocate. That meant I had to find a way to connect and experience joy, right where I was, regardless of what I expected, or had planned, or used to have.

Nature had helped me immensely in the past, so I called on my birds and my trees, and I again received the teaching of impermanence and allowed it to guide me, intuitively, into decisions of housing, neighborhoods, and what California would teach me.

Forgive me if it sounds grandiose for this white lady to say such a thing. It's just the way I talk about the journey. I am better able to frame my journey as an aspirational healing narrative than a story about a disheartened housewife who regrets following her husband. What a relief it is to be here, now, in the middle years when the pressure to conform for the sake of the children, the in-laws, or the husband has softened. I consider birds and trees my true companions, and, as John Prine sang, "Every single blade of grass holds a special place for me." May he rest in peace.

What a joy it is to release what was and understand that the goal is not to remove the grief you touch when you experience the impermanence of all things but to get to know it so that its hold on you lightens and becomes less invasive in the soul garden.

What a joy it is to become conscious that relocating is easy – it's losing one's center of stillness that can prove to be life-threatening.

And while I still have many days of doubt – doubt about my future and the direction of my life and my marriage in these middle years – I have come to accept the doubts as part of my nature, ebbing and flowing like tides. To be more precise, let me add that as we enter the sixth month of the shelter in place for the global pandemic, and massive wildfires engulf the entire west coast of the United States due to climate change, my doubt about all things is flowing.

Sheltering in place was initially what prompted me to write this book; I wanted to share some of the ideas I like to teach, and I couldn't miss the joke the universe was playing, inviting me to slow down and write about moving while being commanded to stay in one place day after day. Turns out, there was never a better time to pen a book about moving, as so many of us are using this time to reevaluate and shift goals, locations and frames for living in alignment with the Earth.

Writing this book provides me a chance to acknowledge the rich friction between begging for mercy and bowing in gratitude and how it has transformed me from a mere mortal, grounded soul who appreciated nature into a soul that can take flight with the birds she befriends and the trees she laughs with. Thank you for letting me share what I have learned with you in the chapters ahead.

And, dear reader, I am still learning.

3

MOVING AS A RITE OF PASSAGE

Since moving temporarily suspends the continuity of one's identity, it is helpful to consider moves as rites of passage. A rite of passage describes what happens when an individual leaves one world, enters a stage of liminality, and then finally joins and expresses a new world. A framework describing rites of passages was presented first by French anthropologist Arnold van Gennep, who lived between 1873 and 1957.

According to Britannica, Gennep's major work was *Les Rites de Passage.* More than a century ago, this brilliant man (who spoke eighteen languages and was, himself, a relocation artist) laid out a framework through which individual transitions from one status to another within a given society could be explained and understood. In ceremonial rites of passage, Gennep discovered that transitions generally followed a three-stage path: separation, transition, and incorporation. He viewed the significance of a rite of passage as a form of reinvention of self within social codes.

The framework describes relocations too. Even if your move is a quick thirty days or less end-to-end, Gennep's three-stage process of separating, transitioning, and incorporating can be used to describe the sacred work of reinvention after relocation.

While checklists and plans are helpful, they capture relatively mundane tasks in the material world. The sacred work of moving is the inner work and rich terrain for exploring meaning. My hope is that you will dig into the inner work of moving – the sacred stuff of self-development and identity transformation you'll be invited into as your next move unfolds. It isn't always pleasurable, but it is highly satisfying.

WHAT I MEAN BY SACRED

I use the word sacred somewhat playfully, not at all in a religious way. Although rites of passage are often related to religious transitions, such as bar and bat mitzvahs, circumcisions, baptisms, matrimonial Rites, or communion, the mover's rite of passage is not religious, though it may open the heart and help you become a more patient person.

For instance, in the last chapter, I talked about the juxtaposition between the expectations I had for our expensive Silicon Valley rental and the reality of it. That discrepancy was painful and disappointing to us. It was also expensive and time-consuming. Working through that adjustment in order to build a peaceful, albeit temporary, home was an invitation for me to persevere, to adjust, and to evolve in ways that taught me to practice gratitude. In this way, the work is sacred because it invites you to revise certain mainstream values and assumptions.

NO TWO MOVES ARE ALIKE

Moving is a "universal" experience, but there are millions of relative experiences that create variety. Since no two people move alike, including two married people, pets, or siblings, the idea of moving as a rite of passage leaves plenty of room for indi-vidual experience, and later in the book, I'll encourage you to write a relocation resumé to help you make sense of your moves. I hope you will.

With this brief description of rites of passage, let's get specific and put it to work for you. I have divided the move into three distinct phases. The first and last stages are the longest and the most diffused as your identity is scrambled, pruned, moved, then replanted in a new place. In this framework, the emphasis is, again, on the inner work of moving. I'll leave the packing of belongings to you and your crew of helpers and friends and give you this loose framework to use as a guide to the feeling side of moving.

PHASE I: SEPARATION (CHAPTERS 4 TO 7)

This phase has you stripping away your former identity and status. While it can be exhilarating to anticipate an upcoming move, for movers who don't have full control over their journey – say they've been laid off or are accompanying a spouse to another location – this initial stage can be filled with anxiety and doubt as you literally shed a former life and lifestyle. A sense of groundlessness can arise, and, with it, you may be tricked into hustling to hurry up and get the move done. But to push for the outer work of moving is to miss the opportunity to separate fully and do the inner work.

The inner work of moving is what Phase I is all about. In the next few chapters, we'll do some exercises that will help you resist rushing and instead cultivate a conscious awareness of where you are today so that you can separate and start contemplating what kind of move you want to make. All feelings are welcome, and you'll learn that you aren't "doing it wrong" if you ride a lot of ups and downs.

As you curate your possessions and make concrete plans for the move, Phase I teaches you how to stay light and present in an expansive way as you open to the future and what your next move has in store.

PHASE II: TRANSITION (CHAPTERS 8 AND 9)

The shortest phase of a mover's work – Phase II takes days or weeks, depending on the complexity of your relocation. The emptier you are emotionally by the time moving day arrives, the easier it will be to move. You will have worked on your resistance in the days or months leading up to the move, so in this short time frame, you will say goodbyes, and "I love you" to help create the sense of an ending.

Ultimately, you'll experience how managing the intangible emotions prior to moving day is important.

PHASE III: INTEGRATION (CHAPTERS 10 TO 14)

The work of Phase III begins the moment your body lands in your new place. Whether you are renting, staying in a hotel or corporate housing, or moving into a home you've purchased, your adjustment starts unfolding, and your brain begins to work hard to make sense of where you are in relationship to where you have been. This is the work of integration (incorporation), and it can take years to complete.

As a sensitive soul who has moved a lot, my Phase III experiences look like success on the outside, but a turmoil on the inside. I've learned that setting up my homes and shelters to look good is important, but that it is the ongoing inner relationship to my environment that ultimately helps me feel at home sooner.

Before we turn the page, I want to share a couple of stories that illustrate how the three phases can unfold differently. Consider Demitria.

Demitria was stuck in Phase I after making a bold decision to move. A single professional woman free from the issues facing an accompanying spouse, Demitria was over-idealizing moving. She was unwilling to engage in the real work of relocation trade-offs, which was disempowering her. While she had a significant budget, her rigid conception of what a "home" should be cost her a lot of energy.

Demetria's fear of missing out on the perfect home belied her down-to-earth nature, and often our work involved resetting to the present moment so that she could get insight into her paralysis. Over a series of conversations, we kept landing back at her childhood home. It was there that the early death of a parent set in motion a narrative about comfort and loss that remained powerfully linked to her notions of home. Without the separation work in Phase I, it will be difficult for her to move without some sort of "let go or be dragged" energy showing up.

Conversely, I am someone who moves almost as if it were an athletic pursuit. I am quick to separate, but I have a much slower attachment to a new place. That is probably why I am such a proponent of using nature as a guide.

Then there are many movers who travel abroad as expats or with the military on assignment. The rhythms and experiences these movers encounter are unique in many ways due to the extra social support, resources, and training they may receive as part of their service program, corporate, or governmental benefit program.

For those of us movers who are less supported by institutions or agencies, I would love to create a ritual acknowledging the stages of moving in the same way many traditional cultures create cere- monies around the hunt or the harvest. Marking the moment would give the relocation artist a chance to earn props and create a shared language around experiences that can be commonly framed, but are wildly varied by things such as taste, personality, culture, economics, or social status.

Wherever you are in your move, I believe that this three-stage frame for understanding moving as a rite of passage – a series of concentric circles that expand outward from separation, to transition, to ultimate integration – can be a helpful support through one of life's most stressful human experiences.

Let's get started with Phase I.

4

THINKING OUTSIDE THE BOXES

"Though we travel the world over to find the beautiful, we must carry it with us, or we find it not."

— RALPH WALDO EMERSON

I n this chapter, you will have an opportunity to separate from where you are today and begin enrolling in your move to the next place. To become conscious about moving is easier said than done because lots of feelings will surface that most of us would prefer to ignore.

I moved so many times I almost felt better when I was in transit from one place to another than when I was awkwardly pausing to say goodbye to friends I loved.

Conscious separating takes practice, and with a

mindful approach it may be much easier on you. Without a mindful approach, you may find that once the moving vans have gone and the pace of activity has quieted down, you could be overcome by the enormity of the changes you've taken on without foresight.

Further, if you are accompanying your spouse on another move, I can guarantee that there are many negotiations between your ego and your soul about who is in charge of this move and why it is the right (or the not so right) thing to do.

I have shortchanged my pre-move mindfulness groundwork in favor of keeping busy and keeping up appearances too many times to mention. That push forward heroism style robbed me of many rich reflections on the miracle of life itself, and I nearly missed how my own humble life was bigger and more interesting to me than I had ever imagined.

Don't jump on that treadmill of constantly looking ahead, ahead, ahead to make sure you aren't losing ground on goals, status, or achievement. Instead, before you start in with your to-dos and running in circles, killing all that awkward time until moving day, I recommend you pause and invest in creating an integrated forward motion toward your next home.

This is the sweetest invitation of moving: pausing. It is a path to greater ease and comfort. I'm gonna put the kettle on, so to speak, and invite you to sit with me like an old friend. I'll write, and you read and let your mind wander.

This should feel safe and simple, like a helping hand, reminding you that while it can be exhilarating to move and restart somewhere new, in this chapter, we are going to cover why Phase I of your move is all about surveying where you are right now with the precision of a scientist and the sensitivity of a poet.

WHERE IS HOME RIGHT NOW? THIS MINUTE?

Try this: Take a gentle breath and allow your gaze to soften into a scene that is somewhere in your home today. When I say home, I mean where you live broadly – your parks, your street, your dirt roads, your high-rise view – whatever place you call home. I promise your home is much, much bigger than your kitchen, your bed, your bath, or your zip code.

When your left brain is in charge, it confines your idea of home to a small unit, and when you are faced with yet another move, the left brain can get pretty noisy.

In this moment, as you take several more centering breaths, begin opening up a connection to the right side of your brain. Let your thoughts travel across the open, creative terrain of the right side of the brain and see what memories of home your sensory body has mapped deeply, even if you are not consciously aware of it.

You will notice a waterfall of place data cascading before you, and it may be highly mundane or exhilarating. Let it flow.

Maybe you get a flash of autumn in the park or the way the blue moonlight travels through your bedroom window. Maybe it's a smell, like the distinctive aroma of orange blossoms from an orchard in the spring, a briny smell at the pier, or the smell of hot concrete cooled by an afternoon shower. Delight in the particularities of the sensory memories you carry.

As you continue to center and gaze at the life bits streaming into your senses, invite more places and more sensory memories in. Go big.

BUILDING A RESERVOIR OF IMAGERY

This exercise can be quiet or riotous, and there is no right or wrong way to experience what you remember. It's all real, all true, and all right, even memories of places you found hard to tolerate and wish good riddance.

Welcome them all and keep pouring the data into a stream for your mind's eye so that this life you have lived – right here, right now – has a vividness that seems extravagant and outsized.

Why should you contemplate your place in the world today with such vividness when you'll be leaving so soon? Because it feels good in the body. Because it feels so good to belong and to know where you are, and the body knows it. In fact, the body works hard to know where it is in time and space.

You must build up a reservoir of imagery that you will call on after the move. As you adjust to your new field of sensory inputs and begin trading off, some trades will be welcome: others will be offensive or disappointing – count on it. Perhaps some of these memory maps you are preparing now will soothe you at those times.

ENDINGS

When you are feeling nourished by this stream of memories and sentiments, go ahead and imagine yourself somewhere in the late afternoon or early evening at sunset.

Can you notice the warmth of the sun as she disappears?

Whether from a bench in Central Park, the water's edge along the Pacific, or out the window from the commuter train you are riding, follow the sun all the way down through the magic hour when it dips below the horizon as the sky remains illuminated. This is the magic hour.

This is the sense of an ending.

This is the softening, the humble vibe of moving. The inner sense of, "What now?" that ushers in an ending while promising a certain hope that tomorrow is another new beginning.

CHASING THE HIGHS

Since we are taught that there is a lot of adrenaline involved in moving, centering down right where you are may cause you to notice, in fact, just how resistant you are to making the separation inquiries.

You might feel that you simply must move along, get going, pack up, and hurry into the work of moving so that you can arrive on the other side, where, the thinking goes, you'll unpack and encounter the reward. But that's the Trickster, not the relocation artist, talking.

Take some time considering the case for moving and what it means to organically and consciously put yourself into a position that literally suspends your identity and changes you in predictable but surprising ways.

WHAT'S YOUR MOVING MANTRA?

I once had a coach who was into mantras. I channeled her on my last move and created a mantra that was based on projecting myself into my next new home. I simply saw myself happily walking brown hills. If it sounds like a downer, it really wasn't. The mantra "brown hills" was strangely befitting.

Anytime friends would ask me, "What are you going to do out there in California?" I would feel somehow at a loss, but I would just dip into my projection and shrug and recite my mantra, "I see myself walking these brown hills."

Was I inadequate because I wasn't teaching yoga or blissing out? At times, I thought yes. But I stayed true, and all I could see was myself walking brown hills that went up and down, and it seemed to me that I was going to be doing it for a while.

I had no idea why I kept seeing myself on these hills, but the vision was benign enough, and I had long since learned to trust what came to me intuitively as a vision because it was always neutral information, neither bad nor good, whose meaning would ultimately be revealed.

Before moving to California, I had only been to San Francisco twice, in the rainy season, and to downtown Los Angeles a couple of times. I hadn't hiked, and I hadn't dreamed of living in California or anything like that. I literally moved blind, so didn't even take the brown hills literally.

I didn't know that the green hills along the peninsula of the San Francisco Bay turned brown in the summer from drought. When, at last, a few weeks after moving, I was invited to hike with my new (and only) friend, Michele, I understood the projection I had been having.

Michele had offered to welcome me to the area after a brief phone call I made to her to check a reference on a property we were considering renting. Michele was serving as our future landlord's reference, so she patiently answered all of my groping questions about the house, the landlord, and the school since she had relocated from the Boston area to Silicon Valley a few years earlier.

Grace was on my side when I was directed to Michele. Besides her being truly one of the most wonderful people in the Valley, she's a relocation artist too. Plus, she is beautiful, she laughs at my jokes, and she is a wonderful cook.

A couple of weeks after moving, Michele invited me out on a hike to Fremont Older, part of the Peninsula Open Space Trust preserve nearby. As she led me up and down the beautiful brown hills all the way to the overlook, the vision came full circle, and I realized that I was suddenly and effortlessly walking the brown hills I had envisioned from my small studio in D.C. as I worked to prepare for the move. It all made sense, and that first flicker of home rippled up in me.

PROJECTION

Somehow, I had "seen" the simple territory ahead without doing much work or research. I used my intuition and inner sensing and discovered a simple story that was benign and caused me no trouble. To this day, I continue to believe "walking up and down" symbolized what to expect from the transition: that my new life would not be flat but would modulate up and down like a wave. As I write this, I am reminded that there have been many ups and downs since arriving in California (as further chapters will explore). For the moment, I'll just note that as I wrote the words "wave" and "modulate," I was reminded that shortly after we arrived, there were a few earthquakes large enough to register. It's amazing how the nonlinear, creative, right, feminine brain uncovers wide intuitive terrain if you let her.

In a later chapter, I'll teach you a technique to help you visualize where you are heading before you arrive so that you have something productive to do with your anticipatory grief. You may already be doing a version of this, unconsciously, as I was.

For now, all I'd encourage you to do is to think outside of the boxes so that you pack up a nice stash of sensory memories culled from your home today, wherever it is, and however you have felt about it. It's early in the process, and you likely have much more time than you realize. Use the open space ahead to keep the concrete to-dos to a minimum and to start dipping into your incredible inward skills. This is the first step in understanding how to enroll consciously in the move ahead.

5

EXPANSIVE ENERGY IS LIGHT

A s you dig further into the separation work, you are creating space to imagine what kind of move you want to make. In this chapter, you'll learn how to seek out expansive energy and why that helps lighten you for the move.

The specific social and gender roles you carry today, prior to your move, will impact how you move. For instance, a mother with young children will separate differently from a single woman stepping into her middle years with a new partner and the colorful sense of adventure menopause brings. Likewise, a single man, long separated from his partner, will have a different point of view about moving than someone who is moving out and on for the first time.

There are literally unlimited versions of moving matters, and it is too much for me to write about as specifically and intimately as I'd like to, but here's a little something to keep in mind: broadly speaking, one of the tricks the mind plays on us when we relocate is crafting an under layer of pressure that feels like urgency to carry on with the dreams we planted in our last place of residence. In a sense, the busy left brain pushes you to deny the enormity of your move so that it can keep its logic together.

Some of the "logic" is social pressure and feels as natural as the air we breathe. For instance, if you have a child with diabetes, it is not optional for you to organize continuous care in your next town so that the child stays healthy. Similarly, pets, school calendars, and drivers' licenses are important.

But what I have seen happen, and I too have experienced, is that because we haven't done the inner work of moving – identifying what kind of move we want to make in this moment – we are at risk of accepting a variety of fairly empty and generic social roles that feel natural in hopes that they'll help us settle in and feel at home sooner. When we do that, we are acting out a false belief that after we move, life will return to some proximation of what it used to be.

This is a mistake that is impossible not to make, so don't worry if you find yourself there right now. The truth about moving is that it's going to change you. Knowing this is frightening but also exciting.

While, of course, it is still possible to pull off life

goals after moving, such as finishing a graduate school degree or continuing to study painting, moving is a nonlinear process. You likely won't hit all of your goals in the straight line (and the narrow timeframe) you were convinced was the right way to do it. Not to worry. Here's a story about one of my favorite friends who paused her painting career several times in order to serve a variety of other goals.

My friend, Yasuyo, is truly a gifted painter. I met her while volunteering at Saratoga High School, where our sons were starting over as juniors.

She had just moved from Taipei in order to accompany her husband on his next job post, and she was staying in a hotel while they looked for a house. Yay, I thought, she is a relocation artist. I loved her immediately.

Yasuyo was so polished and beautiful. Not only was she impeccably pulled together, but her international vibe, sophistication, and elegance also made her irresistible and easy to chat with. I had a hard time pronouncing her beautiful Japanese name at first – which made us both feel awkward – but with practice, I got it and learned that it meant "peaceful era".

She was jet-lagged and living in a hotel, and I was just eight weeks into relocating to California, so the peaceful era was far from reach, as far as I could tell. As seasoned movers, we made an instant connection as we held the door open on the first day of high school registration where we, and our sons, knew not a soul.

In the bright California sun, I sensed she and I both felt the spotlight on our displacement; we were migrants and new to everything, including feeling quite irrelevant since our sons were old enough to want a great deal of space for their own transition.

As we literally stood at the threshold of the school, our boys crossed into young adulthood without us. They were young men who still needed us, but who needed their peers much more. Without a community of friends to support us as we let go of our sons, it was easy for Yasuyo and me to look back and feel homesick.

The initial emptiness after moving often carries some shame and guilt, which triggers attempts to fit in and become invisible. I sensed the same tendencies in Yasuyo that I felt in myself: to fit in and put on an invisibility cloak, at least temporarily. That meant showing up for odd volunteer jobs as needed, but not taking too much of a stake in the surroundings.

Her son had studied at international schools all over the world, and my son attended Sidwell Friends inside the Beltway in Washington, D.C. I was anchored in my diverse community there, and my quirks and history were integrated into all that I did.

Life had a natural flow in spite of challenges and setbacks.

As the school year unfolded, Yasuyo and I settled into a rhythm for our days, and once in a while, we would meet at our favorite cafe, Sue's on Big Basin Road in Saratoga. She would sip on chrysanthemum tea, and I would drink one of their iced yuzu or pomegranate teas.

We were a bit of an odd couple – she an understated beauty, me graying naturally out of frustration that I couldn't find a hairdresser. We were stuck with each other and were well-suited enough to get close in a short period of time.

We would talk about our relocation challenges, our parents, our kids, and our struggles to feel at home in this brand-new world. I am sure you will agree that there is nothing better than finding that first friend after you've moved. Who are the friends that have made your transitions easier? How have you supported each other? Since you never really know how much time you have with a friend, it is important to make time for them.

THE INNER WORK OF MOVING

I want to walk through a series of ideas that I believe will help lighten your load prior to moving. Like all of the inner work of moving, this is intangible stuff, so please pack your imagination with me as you take a couple of breaths and center right where you are into another visualization.

This one is quite different from the exercise in Chapter 4, which was designed to give your sensory body a chance to experience and re-experience all that you have lived, right where you are prior to separating from it.

This next exercise is based on a series of prompts, inviting you to expand yourself as you prepare to move. It's a paradox, right? Moving is about rightsizing and curating your belongings so that you are efficient. Like a .zip file that is compressed by an algorithm prior to transmission, your move is likely to compress you, too.

Take time today to plant two or three inquiries as you go about your day and watch the shift that unfolds. These inquiries are simple, and, when practiced regularly, they can feel like a real break from the chaos and planning for the upcoming move. This is the path to doing the inner work of moving. Simply ask yourself:

- What kind of move do you want to make?
- What is in the way?
- What is a small action you can take right now to release the block and lighten your load?
- What kind of energy feels supportive to you right now?

And listen to what comes up from you. If you are a practiced meditator, work to go deep. If you are new, just simply stay neutral and notice what comes up. I like to call this bird watching; the thoughts and feelings flutter in and out, and some fly while others peck on the ground. Some thoughts are regular – the common birds – some are colorful flights of fancy. All are welcome.

Repeating these four questions helps you return again and again to your relocation artistry:

- What kind of move do I want to make?
- What is in the way?
- What is a small action I can take right now to release the block and lighten my load?
- What kind of energy feels supportive to me right now?

These questions prevent accumulation of sagging energy, the kind that "de-spirits" a mover and sends her on a backward journey looking to identify where she took a wrong turn.

SPIRITUAL MOBILITY, NOT JUST UPWARD MOBILITY

As you practice these inquiries, notice your feeling state. Are you thirsty? Tired? Worrying? Are you distracted? Impatient? Bored? Take a minute to jot a note about yourself on your packing list and let this method help you declutter your possessions, including your spiritual possessions.

In this way, you will find yourself free to create the conditions for spiritual mobility, which is a wonderful companion for upward or outward mobility. I am convinced of this because so many moves, especially relocations in support of a spouse's career, are driven by a presumption of upward mobility and financial success. While upward mobility and professional success are often behind a move, it is also important to unpack what else is going on in a move. In this way, we breathe a little bit more soul into a move.

By focusing on the spiritual side of your relocation, you may keep the flame of pleasure and light alive, which will support you as you lighten your load energetically. You will be surprised to see how these four simple queries can support a variety of self-learning and great self-compassion for the feeling side of moving that is likely to be fairly intense at times.

Now that you have another technique to support you through the separation, let's move into what to do when overwhelm or negativity shows up.

6

CONTRACTIVE ENERGY IS DARK

Shortly after reading Gay Hendricks' book, *The Big Leap: Conquer Your Hidden Fear and Take Life to the Next Level,* I addressed how to stop my addiction to worry, criticism, and blaming my husband for all of our past moves. (Note: My husband might not think I'm completely healed, but I bet if you ask him, he'll say something diplomatic, such as, "She's about 80 percent healed." And guess what? I'll take it.)

I used to be 95 percent addicted to blaming my husband for all of the hardships I faced in our moves to support his career as one of the nation's top photojournalists. There was little room for anything else to grow in my garden with that weed of resentment choking out all the other tender shoots.

Now that I have titrated off of the reactive darkness I carried around for two and a half decades of moving and hustling, I like where I am at today. Why? Because it's simple, and it makes me feel like I can move through challenges and come through to the other side faster – and with friends – because I have integrated the role my spiritual mobility plays in my adjustment to a new city or town.

I value being able to adjust and change as much as I value being rooted and committed and seen as a part of a neighborhood, a community, or a place in the world.

Phase I of the moving right of passage is the part you are most likely to skip because it brings up a lot of discomfort. Notice the tendency to calculate trade-offs that may feel akin to cutting off your nose to spite your face.

A NON-BINARY CHOICE

Who in her right mind would ever choose to leave her best friends in the world in order to live in Paris for five years? You would? Okay, then who in her right mind would hurry home from her well-settled life in Paris just to return to a life surrounded by dear old friends? Oh, you would, right?

Do you see the nature of the dilemma? Relocation is not a binary choice; it's a perfectly imperfect choice that exists within the context of an unlimited number of other perfectly imperfect options. There is no such thing as picking the "best" path; that's a fictitious route. It's about picking a path, period.

In the last chapter, you worked on building up stamina and a process for the inner work of separating prior to your move. The purpose of this chapter, just like the previous two, is to continue to illuminate the idea that energy is what is powering your move and that the better you are at seeking the right energy, the easier your move will be.

SPIRITUAL DECLUTTERING

Since you have moved around a lot, I bet you are skilled at noticing clutter and nonessentials around the house. That might not mean you regularly Marie Kondo your nest top to bottom, but you've gotten some good practice noticing what feels like the right amount of fussy and fancy versus pragmatic perfection in your homes.

But what about your attachments to the status symbols you've achieved where you live today? Maybe you feel you have a prestigious address, and you are heading to a lesser-known or less prestigious zip code. Perhaps you derive your own social status by being part of an elite posse of parents or professionals in a field that has a one-of-a-kind connection to geography. These kinds of attachments I call "spiritual attachments" because they have sustained you in your current life. They are also symbolic and signs of belonging to something. While membership to a religious congregation is also a spiritual attachment, the average life has hundreds of non-religious spiritual attachments at work. During relocation, losing spiritual attachments can contribute to grief, which is why I recommend you start dismantling them in advance with light.

You will want to work on releasing attachments to things that will drain you if you carry them forward. This was one of the hardest lessons for me to learn, and it has also provided some of the most profound insight into achieving greater ease after a move.

The simplicity of practicing affirmations belies their power to influence your life. Affirmations are so powerful because they make us conscious about that which we carry unconsciously; by naming your current spiritual attachments, you are beginning to let them go. This helps you remain relaxed, nimble, and expansive about your move.

The next time you notice you feel distressed about losing status that you view as sustaining and desirable, call the lighter energy forward by growing quiet. Gently affirm one or two of the following statements to start, then let them evolve into highly specific affirmations that speak directly to the attachments that you are most likely to miss when you relocate:

- *Right now, I surrender my power to the simple path that is unfolding before me.*
- *In this season of transition, I'll stay open and let change come through me in creative, just-right ways.*
- *I have everything I need to move safely and serenely while I notice my energy is up and down.*
- *When I notice I am feeling status anxiety about must-haves, don't-haves, and other rigid cords that attach me to material possessions, I will remember to notice.*
- *I will cut the cords tethering me to this place I love, knowing that it is time to go.*
- *I will cultivate my open mind in order to invite the clarity I need to make my new homeplace just right for the next unfolding.*
- *I dismiss blame, shame, and worry because it weighs me down and adds to my burden.*
- *Today, when I notice that I am tired and scared about the future, I will remember to release the spiritual clutter I carry and rest.*
- *Rest is vital to change and growth.*

NEVER GIVE IN TO DARKNESS AND WORRY

Learning not to give your power over to darkness and worry is highly liberating. So is learning how to release the fragments of rogue energy you harbor about your upcoming move – guilt, fear, shame, worry, anger, impatience, or other dark feelings. As you practice surrendering to the light, you will co-create the best conditions for your move. This lightens your load and might even make your move magical.

7

HOW TO THRIVE IN THE THRESHOLD

"But you know, the great thing about liminal space is that it contains the good stuff and it knows what it's doing… Be willing to be. Welcome the surprise of the new arising, the threshold crossing, and the new baby-like state of the fresh self. We are not stuck except for adherence to old left-brain habits, fixed ideas, doubt, and lack of imagination."

— PENNEY PEIRCE, IN HER POST
"LIVING IN LIMINAL SPACE, ENJOYING
THE IN BETWEEN"

The momentum toward your move is likely to pick up dramatically by now. Do you have a firm moving date set? How are you feeling about that? What about housing? Are you the type to lock down a house from afar, or do you like to land and check things out first?

As a review of what we've covered already, we started thinking outside of the boxes so that you could craft a sensory memory inventory (Chapter 4). Then, we introduced queries to lighten your load (Chapter 5) and help keep your energy up. In Chapter 6, we spent a little time on the importance of creating an open and affirming state in the face of worry, self-doubt, and other unsettled feelings that show up on the path to any major move.

With that groundwork laid, now it's time to enter the threshold of your move and begin to uproot yourself from where you are living today and move yourself closer to where you are going – even if you have never been there before.

WHAT IS LIMINAL THINKING?

In Dave Gray's masterful book, *Liminal Thinking*, he lays out a series of lessons and illustrations designed to teach how so-called objective reality is neither objective nor "real" at all. Conditions that appear to us to be impermeable and unchangeable are actually more fluid than we consciously understand. In the chapter "Beliefs Are Created," Gray argues that when one uses liminal thinking to problem-solve, it "requires you to become more conscious of that invisible belief construction process, in yourself and others." Liminal thinking is the art of exploring and using in-between spaces –

thresholds and entryways – to create mindful, positive change.

Since the purpose of my book is not to overwhelm you with cerebral ideas at the moment you are working through the grounded work of separating, I will summarize just a short bit from Gray's book that I believe may help you thrive in the threshold of your upcoming move. I highly recommend his book, as well as any of Penney Peirce's work, as she expertly covers the topics of energy, intuition, and frequency, all important elements to mastering liminal thinking.

If the reality of your life today is being created and upheld by experiences, beliefs, judgments, and theories you hold unconsciously, as Gray argues, then it is easy to see why moving may subject you to a kind of relocation depression. The depression is compounded by the fact that relocation depression, like all depression, is about intangibles seeking expression.

A LANGUAGE FOR MOVING

An unlimited number of intangibles and impermanent bits of data comprise subjective reality when it comes to moving. This makes it difficult to talk about, which compounds the isolation a mover may feel. Since I love metaphors (and trees), I'll try another way to explain the point.

ROOTED TREES ON THE MOVE

If you were a tree, your reality could be considered your root system; the seasons grow you, the animal life you host impacts you, and the forest nurtures you in its network of connected roots. The root system is mature, it is connected, it is complex, and it is underground.

Like a healthy tree that is co-creating the space where it is planted, when you are attached to a place, you are positioned to weather many elements without undue worry for the integrity and stamina of your core root system. You are firmly planted and secure in your home.

Life and her storms will impact you – you'll lose a branch or survive a drought – but the complex of sustaining factors, like the climate and seasons, remain predictable enough that you are able to adjust to hardship. (Although climate change is putting all of life at new levels of risk.)

When you, the tree, are attached and firmly planted, you are at home and stand through a great number of losses and impacts without losing equilibrium.

But say you take a tree out of its home and transplant it far away. You will coax the tree out of its current home, sever its roots, move it across the country, then plant it into new terrain.

In that case, if you want the tree to thrive, you

will need to be much more sensitive to its individual needs and sensitivities, and you'll need to be patient while it adjusts in time to its new surroundings.

Any arborist will tell you prior to transplanting a tree that you must pick the right zone for the tree to thrive, and you must anticipate the extent of new needs the tree will have once situated on its new land.

Since we humans don't come with growing zones, and in most parts of the world moving is common, why aren't we as careful with ourselves as we are with our cherished trees?

EXPLORING LIMINAL SPACE

Liminal thinking is a way to practice moving in your mind without moving your body, and it gives you an opportunity to anticipate and plan for the things you might need when you start unfolding in your new place.

Since your move is approaching, try using liminal thinking to help you consider what it will take for you to thrive in your new locale, even if you've never visited.

Start where you are, and spend some time deeply rooting into your current place. Then, as you begin to feel the pull toward the future, let go and feel your way into the next stop on your journey. By doing this exercise, you are practicing crossing into the threshold from where you are today to where you are going. When you are ready, ask yourself a few questions that may guide you toward information that may be useful to you, even as it comes to you from nontraditional sources:

- *What do you see?*
- *What do you hear?*
- *How do you feel?*
- *Are you alone? Who else is there?*
- *Notice any faces. Are they smiling? Awake? Dull? Joyful?*
- *What other living things surround you?*
- *Are there trees? Insects? Butterflies? Birds?*
- *How are those other living things feeling?*
- *What will you need in your new place in order to thrive?*
- *Is anything missing?*
- *What unnecessary or out of date attachments, relationships, or possessions show up?*

Note any clear information you download while walking through the symbolic doorway from your home today to your home to come. Consider which bits would be useful to incorporate into your moving plans, and which bits seem highly relevant.

By practicing how to explore the idea of home here and home there, you'll diffuse fear and expand your sense of reality. Crossing the threshold of your move will allow you to explore other angles of the move, or even to use this exercise to feel into the experiences other people (or pets) in your circle may encounter in the move. For instance, repeat the exercise, this time asking:

- *What does your [son, daughter, spouse, pet] see in the new location?*
- *What do they hear?*
- *How do they feel?*
- *What expression do you see on their faces?*
- *Are they alone? Who else is there?*
- *What other living things surround them?*
- *How are those other living things feeling?*

PLANTING YOUR SOUL IN TWO PLACES

Remember to be patient as you practice planting your soul in two places, and use this technique anytime you feel disoriented or displaced as moving day approaches. This technique can be useful as you make concrete decisions around schools, houses, apartments, churches, or volunteering. This threshold exercise is also useful after the move whenever you encounter a bout of homesickness or yearning.

Remember the story about my mantra, the brown hills? That was an example of liminal thinking and exploring the threshold prior to a move. I have seen it be extremely helpful to people as they consider accepting a new job and as they are able to embark on a new path with a deep sense of knowing the timing and fit is just right.

One moving client, Jasper, who was extraordinarily sensitive to sound, used this exercise while at open houses, shopping for a new home. In his case, he connected with the house's energy, and, with a little coaching, he was able to pick up on subtle things – the smell of mold, a sagging area of a house, or the lack of enriching sunlight, to name a few things – quickly. This efficiency helped him save a great deal of money. And while his ultimate purchase was much smaller than he envisioned, he is happy at home there.

Thriving in the threshold is useful for any wayfinder or intuitive soul who seeks a deeper level of guidance for decisions around moving than is customarily available from moving companies and packing guides.

8

FAREWELL, GOODBYE, I'M SORRY, I LOVE YOU

W elcome to Phase II of your relocation rite of passage. Like the tree we talked about in the last chapter, you are ready to sever ties and fasten yourself like a healthy root ball wrapped up in burlap so that you can make the safe trip out to your new territory, wherever that may be.

This phase is the shortest part of the moving journey, but it will ask you to produce some of the most sophisticated physical and emotional maneuvers. Don't sweat it; you are prepared, open, and ready to do the tender dismantling of your current identity. It's time.

While the title of this chapter is cute, it is time to honor the finality of your move. Sure, you'll keep in touch, but you will not return to the life you had because both the place and yourself will have changed in subtle and not-so-subtle ways.

Good manners are a big part of this phase, so take a deep breath and rely on simplicity. Fill up your favorite water pitcher and remember that there are lots of us who have been through and are going through the kind of disruptions and dismantling you are in the midst of. You've got this.

The first thing we want to explore is your goodbye style. Answer the following questions:

- Would you prefer a party or a bunch of one-on-one goodbyes?
- Are there a lot of people you have formed emotional bonds with, or are your principal relationships with family members who are moving with you?
- Are you an introvert or an extrovert?
- Are you friends with people across ages, stages, or preferences that celebrate the same way?
- What kind of energy feels right to mark the occasion of your departure?

You get the idea. These kinds of queries will help put clarity around how you unfold your goodbyes and how your friends are likely to bid farewell.

RECONCILIATIONS

On a more somber note, moving often brings the occasion to say I'm sorry to someone you have hurt, or to forgive someone who's hurt you.

In my last move, I felt sad leaving my father, who was sick and housebound, and who I believed was close to dying. It was just a sense I had. For the last couple of years of his life, I visited him almost weekly, so I didn't feel as though I abandoned him. But in fairness, he had advanced multiple sclerosis (MS) and was confined to a scooter where he lived on campus at an independent living facility we had moved him into in order to be closer to us. The timing of our move was not ideal.

My moving away meant that my sister would need to pick up some of the visitation needs my absence left unmet, and since she lived a bit farther away from our father, that meant a lot more traffic and time from her.

When he died six months after I moved, even though I fully expected his imminent passing, my grief compounded my adjustment to my new home.

Still, I was thankful that he passed because it would have been terribly burdensome on my sister if our father's poor quality of life continued. His suffering was heartbreaking to us all in his later years as his quality of life eroded from three decades of MS and the secondary mental health issues it caused.

Thank you, dear sister, for still wishing me well when you knew, in my absence, you would have more to do. I'm sorry I wasn't there for you, and I still miss you every day. I am happy you let me clean his place out all by myself. That gave me a great deal of joy since he never wanted us in his space.

I mention this story to you, dear reader, because sometimes we are so caught up in the forward momentum of our move that we forget that our absence will impact others who love, care, or depend on us. I recommend spending some time reflecting on those relationships and putting some language on the issues that come up. It is always the right time to reach out to a friend, lover, sister, or brother to tell them how much the time you had together meant and that you were sorry you had to leave so soon.

WHO ARE YOU LEAVING BEHIND?

Is there someone in your place today who will be impacted by your move? Is there a conversation to have to acknowledge that? It may take only ten minutes, but it helps you set the stage for a lighter move, knowing that your unfinished business is tended to.

In some cases, especially when you are an accompanying spouse, the person you may need to forgive is yourself; feeling guilty and like a failure for being dependent on your spouse is an out-of-date frame through which to consider the complexity of family dynamics on the move.

You might also need to forgive friends who may have complex feelings about your moving. Because I have moved so much, I am sensitive to others leaving too.

Remember Yasuyo from Chapter 5 – the new friend I made just weeks into my life in California? Well, approximately twenty months into our friendship, she unexpectedly moved to Europe with just thirty days' notice. I could have cried when she told me.

It was a shock for her, and it sent shockwaves through me too as I watched her start working her relocation artistry. As I type this out, Yasuyo is adjusting to the pandemic from a new home in Europe while grieving the loss of her father, who died in Japan just as she left California. Luckily, she made it to his bedside prior to his passing.

As for me, I am mourning the loss of my beautiful local friend and the style and understanding she brought to our coffee chats. I miss her.

Life continually moves forward, and, as often as I have left important relationships and places, I have not been spared the other side. We all get plenty of turns being left and feeling bereft. Who knew we'd get so much practice setting our loves free?

I LOVE YOU

Now it's time to talk about everyday love: the kind of effervescent love that is not quite an emotional affair but is racy and lovely and is hard to let go of when it is integrated into one's day. Why do I want to talk about this? Because you may find this variety of love hard to replicate where you are going, at least initially.

I was crazy about my last two butchers, and I have yet to fall in love with my butcher here in California. Similarly, finding chemistry with couples that works all four ways is not as easy at fifty as it is when you are a youthful thirty or forty with lots of time and interest in mixing out and about. It takes time to reinvent yourself in your new place, so before you go, be sure to let everyone you've loved know how much they meant to you.

By saying, "I love you," you will remember what kinds of friends you are attracted to, and it also allows you to update your friend group, which is critical as your values and goals and needs evolve with age.

I loved my postman, the man who drove the snowplow, and the housekeeper I had. I loved neighbors, teachers, and friends, and I made a point of telling as many of them that I could.

I LOVE YOU WITH FRIENDS

We had a whole six months (almost too much time) to dismantle our life in D.C. prior to moving to California.

Because we had raised our kids there, my good-byes and "I love yous" centered on my amazingly talented mom friends, my neighborhood friends, friends that were couples, and friends that I loved but didn't quite fit into any group.

I find myself taking a deep breath as I sit here to write further about this moment because, nearly three years later, I can still touch the grief of friendships suspended.

Saying goodbye was difficult. I could see the empty nest approaching, and I wanted to dig in and get back to long-held dreams and ambitions I had put on hold for a couple of decades. I didn't want to make all new friends at fifty. This was my tribe, and I hated leaving it, knowing I would have to start over in a new place.

Since I didn't have the words to express my love for some of my special friendships and mentors, I came up with an art project to help express myself. Here's a story about how I solved my goodbye problem. I offer it to you in hopes that it inspires you to craft a similarly expressive and personal farewell.

A TRIBUTE TO THE GROUND WE WALKED
TOGETHER

As I thought about the friends who touched me deeply over my D.C. years, I wanted to pack them up with me: memories from their kitchen tables, long walks along the canal, and dance moves we shared in the wee hours. What could I buy that reminded me of our years together, raising kids while feeling like it uniquely expressed me? Turns out, nothing.

I mused on the idea of capturing the ground we walked together, and then I had a flash of insight: I would collect soil samples from some of our common territories and see what the color variety looked like. If it was interesting enough, I would grind the different soils into separate pastes and make a soil rubbing onto fine paper. If you would like to see how the project turned out, I've posted a link to the project and photos in the Resources section of the book.

When I had completed rubbing the soil of nine meaningful locations I had shared with friends, I scanned the original twenty-inches-by-thirty-inches piece then had twenty smaller, ten-by-sixteen-inch prints made on watercolor paper. On the back of each little poster, I wrote my friend a goodbye love letter of gratitude as a tribute to the ground we walked together. I packed each one in a manilla envelope and spent time delivering and saying goodbye, one on one.

I was deeply touched when I learned that a few of my friends framed their prints and put them on display in their office or home. It made me happy to know that a little part of me was continuing to be a part of them after I moved away. I took a little bit of them with me, too, as the original soil rubbing hangs in my new house as a wonderful reminder of our D.C. years.

MAKING IT UP AS YOU GO ALONG

By putting language or a visual on the passages you live through, you are empowering yourself to feel less intangible, less invisible, and more at ease in spite of the moves.

You will have also shown up for your goodbye in a way that helps you get that at-home feeling sooner because you held nothing back. Sometimes it won't feel as pleasurable as I just described. Sometimes it will not feel good, even if it is right.

GOODBYES COME IN ALL SHAPES AND SIZES

When I was younger, I hated goodbyes. I thought they took too long, and I also felt ill-equipped to master all of the uncomfortable, awkward, time-sucking in-between feelings that bombarded me at parties or family gatherings.

Alcohol helped make it easier to slip out the back door in an Irish goodbye or to endure uncomfortably long hugs from people I may not have been prepared to touch.

Today, in my early fifties, goodbyes are less awkward, and they are often tinged with a bit of melancholy, knowing that life moves us in vast ways and that sometimes goodbyes are final. The current pandemic has been a cruel teacher of finality and change.

But even now, with the world locked down and America confused, there is always a sweet reward when one remains conscious and allows one's soul the chance to be raw and a bit laid out in a goodbye.

Don't be fooled into thinking goodbyes are straightforward. They are not. Goodbyes come in all shapes and sizes.

Recall the goodbyes you've endured or initiated. Which side would you rather be on? The side of saying goodbye or the side saying farewell?

How have your past goodbyes gone? Were you able to "keep in touch" or did the relationship settle into a simple social media post exchange? I find all the varieties of change in my relationships after relocation, and it is a wonderful surprise to see how connections shift in time. Some friends have drawn closer to me and I to them, while other friendships gently fade in time.

A CHILDHOOD GOODBYE

I remember one truly tender goodbye I shared with a dear friend, Kay. We were fourteen years old, and it was sunrise at the intersection of Bridle Path and Main Street in our tiny town, just three-square miles in area.

In the early morning light, we hugged and said we'd promise to write. I was heartbroken and envious too. How exotic it must be to move. I wanted to know all about it.

She was not only moving; she was going to boarding school, something I thought I should do since I loved school and was good at it. I didn't understand why I couldn't go. (I later learned that the expense of it was a nonstarter for my parents.)

This was a formative memory, and I believe that somehow I was being invited to consider how moving was linked to educational opportunities and the chance to have a more exciting lifestyle. It's no wonder I married a guy who attended boarding school and who has kept me moving from the moment he said hello!

But the story does not end at fourteen, dear reader. Forty years after saying goodbye to someone or someplace you have loved in a formative way, you too may have a chance to welcome the person or place back. And what a homecoming it can be!

That's why I encourage you to write your story in pencil, so to speak, as the worlds we leave are often returned to us anew over the course of a lifetime. That's what ran through my mind when Kay and her family showed up for a visit this year on the occasion of our daughters attending the same college, just a few miles from our new home here in California.

The lighter I learn to hold reality, the easier I find it is to play with.

THE BEGINNING OF THE ENDING

Every goodbye is different and can be a portal to your Phase II experience. Remember, this is the stage when you are likely to feel suspended and identity-less in some ways. One thing I have experienced as I have stretched goodbyes out through Phase II of a move is how immaterial so many of my concerns and preoccupations were. I also learned that there is a finality to leaving a place that bears honoring, even as paths may cross again and you plan to visit.

If you find this chapter a bit tricky, consider it an invitation to feel your way through the awkward interior of farewells; not quite knowing what to say, to do, or who to be provides a great deal of space for what is real and true to emerge. The in-between states can be a place to rest up before moving day.

9

MOVING DAY: DRAMA OR DHARMA?

"'Where are we going to move to?' Brother asked.

'To the valley,' said Papa as he began putting lamps and things into a box.

'The valley?' said Brother. The valley down there was nice to look at, but he wasn't so sure he wanted to live there. It was so far away."

— *THE BERENSTAIN BEARS MOVING DAY*, STAN AND JAN BERENSTAIN

That final forward motion has arrived, and with it, you, your loves, your curated possessions, your pets, and spirits will move ahead in faith and hope, jumping into a future with open hearts and tired bodies. While you won't be moving into a cool treehouse in the valley, like Brother from the Berenstain Bears children's book series, your move is still going to be a big adventure, filled with surprises and, naturally, a few disappointments and temporary setbacks.

ARE YOU READY?

If you have been practicing techniques from the earlier chapters, you might be feeling a bit more expanded; a little lighter and more prepared and centered for the uncertainty that lies ahead.

If you have moved a great deal, especially in support of your spouse's career, you may start to recall past traumas and losses on moving day. This is natural, and be sure to take extra care of yourself. My experience has taught me that the work gets done and that the gentler you are with yourself, the greater endurance you are able to sustain.

A BALANCING ACT

The moment of moving calls us into a balancing act whereby we let ourselves simultaneously feel the polarities of moving: the uncertainty on the one hand and the expectancy on the other. We can work with the two polarities in a way that helps us deepen our acceptance of impermanence while reducing extra stress and friction as the circus of moving makes a juggling act for us.

To be clear, I am not a Buddhist. Rather, like

many American mindfulness practitioners, I borrow from all sorts of traditions in my practice. However, there are many useful teachings from Buddhism that have helped me move and process my moves.

One such teaching comes from vipassana meditation and its emphasis on living the dharma in daily life.

WHAT IS THE DHARMA?

According to Philip Moffitt, a founder of Spirit Rock Meditation Center, Dharma means "truth" or "the way things are," and it also refers to the teachings of the Buddha. While there are various interpretations of the term, Moffitt uses it to describe the application of spiritual insight to finding freedom and well-being in your daily life, just as it is.

In the moment of moving, your daily life is scrambled beyond recognition, as are many of the quiet centering routines you might call on to keep you feeling calm or less anxious. Your daily life is temporarily suspended and out of reach, and noticing that is where the magic is.

Time will slow down with this awareness, and you may find that you are filled with a sense of wonder and curiosity rather than overwhelm. When you go deeper into this reflection, you may touch an experience I can only describe as dissolution of self.

While you may still feel fragmented by a whole

range of emotions – sadness, fear, anger, and confusion – when moving day arrives, by now, you understand that linear forward motion is propelling your change. You will want to simultaneously rely on the forward motion while opening up to the dissolution of what was, what was once, and what used to be.

While your boxes are loaded up and your furniture is moved, see if you can bring unity to the masculine and feminine principle amidst the chaos. Allow the two forces to work in concert and move you.

What I am encouraging you to do is to observe the polarity between the feminine impulse to root down, convene, and stick together in community and the masculine line of the arching arrow moving forward into new territory.

It's classical pas de deux, a partner dance, even as gender roles in marriage become more fluid and less socially prescribed. The energetic principals of the masculine and feminine persist in balance, and you are well-equipped to play all the parts in the dance of your move. Continue to meet each contraction of energy on moving day with a breath that opens and expands you forward. Be lifted up by the masculine and soothed and held by the feminine.

WHAT TO DO WHEN DRAMA SHOWS UP

I will only cover a bare minimum about what I call
"drama moves" and why they should be avoided at
all costs if possible. I resist writing much about this
because there is already plenty of cultural reinforce-
ment for drama in moving, and it is presented to us
as the norm in the media and through lore. Moving
nightmare stories are everywhere. If you don't know
what I am suggesting, just go hang out at the truck
rental counter, or at a box place, a storage facility, or
a shipping store. You'll hear all you need to about
rip-offs, delays, long waits, high prices, and useless
red tape.

I've experienced drama moves too. They come in
all shapes, sizes, and budgets. The easiest way to
prevent a drama in moving is to take good care of
yourself and make sure that you are well-rested,
hydrated, and healed for the move ahead. If you are
moving after a loss of any kind, preventing a drama
move is easier said than done because your raw feelings are likely to surface if the logistics falter.

If you aren't ready to move and you can postpone
in order to set up more support or to address that
"something's not quite right" feeling within, do it.
It's not too late to make adjustments. If it is not
possible to inquire and postpone, just prepare to be
exhausted, and do the adjusting on the other side of

the move (when you'll have plenty of other adjustments to make).

I've been there.

A FOREMAN GOES MISSING

I once had a moving crew that was kind but incompetent. They showed up to our house a half-day late
after commuting from three states away. The
foreman went missing. When he finally did show up
for his crew, he didn't have packing supplies, and his
truck was too small. All of our items were packed
and then tied up on top haphazardly for a cross-
country move.

I didn't trust this guy, and I didn't respect him. I
was merely wholly dependent on him. This had me
feeling vulnerable and scared on moving day, a
perfect storm for a drama move.

As gender issues and power dynamics tripped us
up, the process of packing up, which took place in
record heat, became highly charged and personal.
Brooks tried to protect us, but he had been working
offsite, so didn't know the details the way I did. Plus,
he was enraged, and I worried things would come to
blows.

We needed a lot of help. There was more
complexity to the move than most because our
belongings would be dropped to two different locations, both across the country. It didn't matter that

we had already discussed the complexities ad nauseam in the planning stage; without a foreman directing the crew, we were going to miss our deadlines and likely some possessions too.

Nobody wanted me in charge, including me, but that's what I did – I took charge. It was awful, especially because we were told the company provided so-called "white glove" service to its relocation clients. Brooks was as shocked and disappointed as I was.

As an empath, I was picking up on gender issues, social class issues, educational issues, and the sheer truth that these men – in our case, they were all men – were extremely hard-working and honest, but they had no manager to serve them. As hard as I tried to be upbeat and organized, the enormity of the move pulsed dark energy through me. Between the language barrier and a literacy barrier, I couldn't read the labels scratched illegibly onto the boxes. What else could I do but make sure I knew what was what amidst all of the boxes?

Looking back, I should have pulled the plug and rescheduled the move by a couple of days. We couldn't do that without a lot of fallout, but nothing is worth adding drama to moving day. If things aren't quite right, stall or delay until it is clear how to move forward without drama.

The last thing I should have tried to do was play foreman and do the final dismantling of my life in such an unsupported way. I was pulled in a million directions while worrying nonstop about the well-being of myself, my family, our possessions and the crew. The smartest thing I did was to go upstairs, curl up into a ball of unpacked bedding, and treat myself to a major, chest heaving, existential cry.

YOUR LIFE, JUST AS IT IS

There is little else to say about moving day. Even if drama shows up, you'll manage. Your arrangements and expectations will hold up for you, and, if they do not, you will adjust and manage as the relocation artist the world is asking you to become. It may not be pretty, but it will still be moving day and both a reflection of your current reality and a chance to check in on how you are tending to yourself.

Don't believe all the advertisements and the urgency. There is no absolute timeline you must adhere to in order to meet objectives; a plan is just a good guess at a moving target (pun intended). There is no need for overly rigid to-do lists; there is just a box at a time and the invitation to stay present and humble to the idea that you are in the process of becoming someone new.

In conclusion, drama happens when a circular emotional current overpowers the linear plans put in place, and you can't manage logistics. This kind of overwhelm adds a hefty tax to moving day, but it can still be a learning experience.

Ideally, you will have a more serene, mindful moving day which flows. While it may be chaotic and require a lot of grounded, physical work, it will also be tactical and linear, built on trust, and able to buffer the unexpected (and expected) trip-ups, such as last-minute questions, a broken item or two, tears of farewell, and sometimes, but rarely, a white-gloved foreman gone missing.

10

LANDING IN A NEW PLACE

"I have learned that my home, my country, is the whole planet Earth."

— THICH NAT HAN

As you step around empty boxes poised for recycling and, like a set designer, quickly find just the right place to pose your sweet desk and chair, your favorite *objets d'arts*, and your family photos, your subconscious goal is just to hurry up and feel at home fast.

I say slow down.

Just as you worked through Phases I and II, let's consider the old gardener's bit; it describes Phase III of the relocation passage perfectly. Gardeners recite this ditty when they want to capture what happens after planting a new garden:

First year it sleeps, second year it creeps, third year it leaps.

Isn't this a wonderful phrase to keep in mind for unpacking in a new location?

With time stretching out before you in such an open-ended way, the question becomes: how would you like to spend that first year? It requires being relaxed and efficient so that you can nourish all of the traits you cherish in yourself and want to seed in your new place. This is how we unpack the soul first:

- Slow down so that you can attach to the Earth.
- Notice the climate and how different it feels to your body.
- Notice the shelter you've landed in; how does it make you feel? What is it "saying" to you?
- What does the water taste like in your new home?
- What about your first impression of the neighborhood? Besides being different, can you describe any differences in detail?
- How about nature? What is the geography of your new place?

As you survey your new place, resist the temptation to compare if at all possible. Keeping with the open, just-as-it-is, impressions of your life, let the new terrain spark your curiosity and your growth one day at a time. Slow down and start quietly mapping your new homeplace.

THIS IS WHERE YOU BELONG

In Melody Warnick's book, *This Is Where You Belong*, she walks through in detail her adjustment to Blacksburg, Virginia, after her husband accepts a position at Virginia Tech, and the family relocates from Austin with two school-age daughters in tow.

It's a wonderful book, and I hope you'll pick up a copy. You'll appreciate Melody's candidness and her smarts. Plus, you'll likely learn a great deal about placemaking: the art of designing the public spaces that residents of contemporary urban neighborhoods crave. It's a primer in urban planning and is fascinating, especially to me, someone who is interested in the creative ways we adjust when accompanying a spouse on a big relocation.

In my book, I am using the term placemaking to describe the process an individual, not a city, uses to curate an attachment to a new place. For instance, when I started placemaking in San Jose, my favorite thing to do was to step out the front door and just start walking without a map. All I did was look around and notice my surroundings.

Maybe it sounds like a glorified way of being lost, but, as the saying goes, not all who wander are lost.

The only way this sister feels grounded and at ease is through deepening her connection to the soil, so, intuitively, my adjustments begin with walking.

Sure, I got myself turned around and a bit uptight when dark was falling, but the payoff was that I felt at home faster. I didn't need to rely on online map services or my hubby or new neighbors with deep roots. It was important to me to recognize where I lived and to begin building my sensory memories up immediately. Plus, I was able to map so much more detail about my surroundings by putting one foot in front of the other. I hope you'll try it too.

PLACEMAKING WITH DAD

I moved for the first time as a kid at seven years old. We moved from a tiny suburban Levitt House in Nassau County, New York, out to the unsettled east end of Long Island, in Suffolk County. It was the country.

Our new house was a contemporary complete with a lot of glass, a Japanese Garden, and a cool, gravel driveway. I was shocked by the quiet and the way the meadows expanded between houses. It also felt confusing that a beautiful new home could feel so lonely. Where were all the kids in the neighborhood? It was so quiet. I missed my crew. Thankfully, my dad noticed.

Before MS took the use of his legs, he used to

invite me bike riding from time to time. One day, he told me to follow him, and we'd go out looking for friends. I was ecstatic. I had to ride a couple of miles uphill, but, at seven, I could do it, no problem, especially if it meant I might make a friend.

I never pedaled faster, and I recall it like yesterday the miracle of spotting that Woodie station wagon loaded with kids in sandy bathing suits on their way home from the beach. Jackpot! My dad flagged them down and introduced us. He said we were new to the village and were out "looking for friends." It was magic and the beginning of the extraordinary lifelong friendship I have built with my soul sister, Kimberly. Thank you for teaching me how to go out looking for friends, Dad.

What about you? How do you like to make friends? Is there a story that you like to tell about how you made your first friends when you were new to a place? What kind of environments help you step out and make friends?

WHEN YOU ARE LOOKING FOR FRIENDS AT FIFTY

Not much has changed for me since I hit the friend jackpot at seven, really. I'm still out looking for friends in new places. The difference is that now I'm in my fifties, and I am much more selective about who I enjoy spending time with. Although part of me would still like to jump on a bike with my dad and start waving at cars full of people, the art of making friends at fifty is pretty similar to what it was at seven: find a way to put yourself out there and be receptive to what shows up. It's birdwatching, really.

This is how I met my soul sister, Eliza, in Cambridge, Massachusetts: waiting at the bus stop for the number seventy-two up Huron Avenue into Harvard Square.

This is how I met my beautiful friends Lori, Lisa, and Eva, at the art studio here in San Jose. Lisa and Eva kindly invited us to Thanksgiving when we were new to town.

Writing and reflecting on friendship is so poignant. I need friends to manage the kind of spread my life has today and to balance the outer trappings of life in the middle years with the inner awakenings and the tiny gems of wisdom that these years offer.

In terms of making friendships with women in their fifties, I say fret not. As the nests empty and we enter our juicy middle years, women are renewed, open, and alive to forming relationships based on interests and common values rather than on prescribed social roles and neighborhood or social circles formerly driven by the children or the spouse.

Go ahead in that new town; tap dance, host a podcast, join a women's circle, start a garden, chat with your neighbors, get a puppy, save the trees, get sober, take up painting, get your first job, or leave your job behind for good. Whatever you do, do it slowly and do it with pleasure. Placemaking with new friends will happen in time.

IN THE MEANTIME, LET YOUR INTUITION GUIDE YOU

The last part of this chapter is probably the most important to unpacking your soul first when you land in a new place.

As you know, the chores and to-dos to resettle are extensive, so as you prioritize what you want to do and when, consider that your new place is calling you to engage with it in a certain way. If you learn how to tune into this, you will feel ease much faster.

For example, when we moved from Boston to D.C. six months after 9/11 so that Brooks could cover the White House for *Time* magazine, we had a one-year-old and a three-year-old. One of the first things I had to do was find a new pediatrician.

Back then, health plans used to publish these giant directories of health care providers by specialty. The directory I used showed credentials but no photos or educational information, so it was basically like buying wine by the label. Since I didn't know my way around town well, I tried to gauge convenience to the office as one of the top criteria for selection. I didn't even think about race or gender, at least not consciously.

What a surprise it was to me that I kept selecting pediatricians who were Black and Brown People of Color out of the generic preferred providers list. After meeting with the first two, I thought their offices were too far across town and, therefore, too hard to get to during commuter hours. But I didn't miss what my city was teaching me; I was being led into a bigger realm of diversity.

When I brought the kids into the third pediatrician practice, this one just a mile from our house, and she too was a talented and accomplished Black woman, that was that. For the next fifteen or so years, in spite of the outrageously long waits she was famous for, the doctor and her team of talented female pediatricians and administrators loved and took good care of the children (their mother too).

While this story may seem an overly simple example of unconscious racial bias, I share it here because it represents the kinds of subtle challenges to your status quo you are likely to encounter in your move. Racial bias is hard to talk about and the farther from home you go, the more likely your biases will come into stark relief. Start practicing and consider yourself lucky to evolve.

GET TO KNOW YOUR BIASES

To have a bias or a sense of preference is human, but you must recognize and own up to said biases when they block you (or another you meet) in your new place. Address them and continue to grow into the beautiful soul you are meant to be by opening up to new things.

The biases that surface in a move won't always be racial; often, your biases will show up around areas such as class, education, rural vs. urban, religious preferences, style of dress, or the type of automobile one drives. Occasionally, shifting your biases will feel challenging, but most of the time, at least from my perspective, the opportunities to grow far outweigh the discomforts.

As biases and preferences come up, look for the opportunity to name them, heal them, and either let them go or transform them in time. Upgrades are always right on time, and I highly recommend building your proximity to diverse support systems as a path to settling in faster. Doing so will support your growth and authenticity as someone who can manage all kinds of situations with grace and gratitude.

Wherever you have landed, the place and the people you meet will have countless stories to share. Let them. Your intuition, as well as your eyes, ears, heart, soul, and imagination, will guide you to the stories and transformations you and your family need most.

SHEDDING MORE OF YOUR POSSESSIONS

After the move, you may find that you need to let go of not only a bunch of bias, but even more of the things you've brought. Somehow we always have too much.

When I came to California, I had so many beautiful East Coast clothes. Little by little, I have been shedding them to the local shelters or the thrift shops as my new life unfolds. I think of myself like a tree that is defoliating in a particular season. I am still the same tree; it's just a season of loss. I've used that metaphor countless times to help me create ease in my new home sooner.

There is a great deal of conscious give and take that you'll begin as soon as you land. This is the beginning of grieving what you've lost and the ease with which you may have lived prior to relocation. This is all part of the journey, your relocation rite of passage. What about you? How can you tap into your intuition and create metaphors of meaning?

Can you notice patterns where you've just landed? What do they mean? How can they help you way-find? I use these questions to help me unlock what is magical about a place.

Keep discovering.

11

WHERE THERE'S GRIEF, THERE'S GROWTH

"Though we do not wholly believe it yet, the interior life is a real life, and the intangible dreams of people have a tangible effect on the world."

— JAMES BALDWIN

In this chapter, I am going to do a deep dive into grief and why it is ultimately the relocation artist's superpower. Even as I write this, I am tempted to oversimplify and write a neat and tidy paragraph that lays out the path forward through grief after a move. Nonsense. Grief will have its way with us however it pleases, and it's rarely a straight line.

While there is no one-size-fits-all plan to relocation grief, there is a need to be open to it and to have resources that touch your heart and bear witness to you as you feel feelings. This chapter will help you get started.

When you and your family are adjusting to a new place – especially if the move was triggered by a job loss or a financial necessity you had no control over – processing your individual and familial grief is a practice that, when given lots of room, surely strengthens compassion and tolerance for self and others. It takes time, and doing the work is entirely optional.

Many serial movers show up as I did for years, operating as if not much has changed in the relocation. As if, once the house is set up and the shell of a normal routine is established, all is well … I didn't know better.

I continued to invest in the narrative that I, the marriage, the kids, and our mutual career goals were all unfolding as planned and that all was just fine. "Yeah, I'm good. I swapped this house for that house. I swapped this market for that market, this school for that," and I would go on and on. Inside, I was still crying about things I left behind, the new challenges I couldn't face and felt ill-prepared to address.

The all-is-well story can work for a long while, but at some point, the moves will catch up to you, and you'll be invited to do the integration work. You may prefer to do the work privately, but I don't recommend putting this phase on hold.

If you decide to carry on with the stiff upper lip, how can I judge you? Alas, I've been there.

If you aren't ready to deal with the Phase III Integration work and conversations about grief, I get it. You are still so beautiful, and your moves are magical, and I love you madly.

Let's connect someday.

If, however, you are ready to "go there" and have stockpiles of losses in line for metabolization, let's get started.

THE TRAUMA OF ORDINARY LIFE

By now, you know that I am biased and that I believe lives unfold in an organic, strangely beautiful process, one that integrates light and dark in balance according to some mythological recipe we have yet to discover. I believe that every life is composed of myriad ups and downs, lows and highs, and often the switch-ups come without warning.

I continue to be surprised by the extent to which every single life story carries trauma beyond expectation and stories of resilience in equal measure.

From broken dreams, addictions, poverty, criminality, affairs, abandonment, divorce, death, loss, longings, unemployment, homelessness, infertility, incarceration, or suicide, the ways we suffer may be unique, but that we suffer is universal.

As far as life's problems (with a capital P),

moving is typically relegated to the bottom of the list. It's considered a common life problem, like the hassle that comes with painting the house. I think this myth misses the mark.

Moving may be ordinary, but it is also extraordinary. Check the language we use to talk about relocation, for instance: it's "a tough transition" but "often worth it." We speak about moving with broad strokes, as I have noted earlier, which lends the impression that relocating is a mere lightweight kind of trauma to endure, a linear journey.

To any man or woman who has lived multiple relocations from the inside out, moving homes, lives, careers, and children is a much more nuanced challenge than we have language for. This is why we default to good and bad and other binary, laundry-sorting kinds of summaries about our moves instead of feeling the feelings and becoming conscious of the trade-offs.

Further, when certain life goals advance in a move, say a salary increases, the family lands a bigger home, or someone receives a more prestigious title, the guilt of feeling bad inside seems like a disconnect with "the good life" earnings on the outside. It's tempting to try to keep up appearances, a strategy that may work temporarily, but it leads to a lot of blocks long term.

What to do when the lack of language presents a problem for you? When the paradox of moving's "ups and downs" feel like trauma? The first step is to expect this to happen and to give yourself permission to start a conversation about any and all feelings relocating brings up in you. You aren't alone.

RELOCATION ARTISTS KNOW A BIT

One of the things that a true relocation expert understands is that keeping up appearances blocks adjusting to all the changes facing you in your new life. They know that practicing how to grieve with authenticity and style helps keep them together and forward-looking, which often attracts the best kind of new friends. The modern moving strategy is to be as stylish with your grief as your home décor and to incorporate it into your story while blending other aspects of yourself into the story as well.

Let's consider Jackie Kennedy Onassis, one of our great relocation artists who was also an accompanying spouse. (Michelle Obama is another example.) Jacqueline "Lee" Kennedy Onassis was born in Southampton, New York, back when the Hamptons were rural, horsey, and artsy.

Imagine yourself in Jackie's beautiful shoes as you consider the lengths she ultimately went to in order to support her husband and family. She was the mother of two young children and the accompanying spouse to an ambitious politician, and it is miraculous how steadfastly and elegantly she accompanied John Kennedy on their truly one-of-a-kind journey while maintaining her status as a fashion icon. How was she able to stay steady through all of the fragmentation she endured?

Imagine Jackie and contemplate how her husband's betrayals must have compounded her challenges after all she did to support his profile as complete and powerful.

By age thirty-four, this accompanying spouse had lived up and down the East Coast, traveled on the campaign, been First Lady, birthed three children, lost one of them, become a widow, and the life she had helped create became diffused. She never sought the spotlight, yet found herself squarely in it until her death, even as she dismantled and rebuilt herself many times.

Tragically, Jackie was present in the motorcade at the moment of her husband's assassination. Her grief from losing baby Patrick Bouvier Kennedy just prior to the assassination apparently merged with her grief for her husband as she went from First Lady to widow and mother to two small children.

Can you feel this quiet patriot's longing for inner peace?

I am humbled thinking about the multitude of layers of grief Jackie humbly experienced and inte-grated into her life and character from her quiet perch on the Upper East Side after the Washington, D.C. years. She and her two young children will always be America's iconographic (privileged, white) family in grief: stoic, well dressed, and mythologically American.

TIMES HAVE CHANGED

I admire Jackie even as I mourn the full-throated expression of her voice, one which we never got to hear. In her later years, while she became an editor, her voice remained behind the scenes, almost as a whisperer of good works – the books, the civic projects, and the advocacy for public parks and architecture. What treasures she oversaw for public benefit.

Jackie has always been a wonderful role model to me, but it is only in writing this humble book that I started to see how she put grief to work in the world in order to manage it. She continued to work for beauty, for the public good, and for public parks and civic enhancements long after she was thrust unexpectedly out of the White House. While surely none of us is Jaqueline, positioned to walk into high profile volunteer assignments when we are in a new place, many of us can learn how to put grief to work for us in service to a higher goal.

As much as I admire Jackie, when contextualizing her life choices today, she is somewhat of a model for the submissive accompanying spouse of her era. Most contemporary spouses would agree that her approach is a bit too one-sided, a bit too pro-husband for our times. Fortunately, we have another First Lady who was in office more recently: Michelle Obama. Michelle updated the role with contemporary language and action from day one on the campaign, and continued to do so all the way to the White House.

BECOMING LIKE MICHELLE

In her book *Becoming*, Michelle Obama gives us a lot to chew on when she writes about accompanying her spouse on the campaign. She invites us to come a little closer to what it felt like to be in her position and to consciously trade-off and postpone her career goals in support of her husband, family and the nation.

A brilliant and accomplished woman, Michelle, like Jackie, is a fashion icon and is one of the most popular people in the world today. She was (and is) unjustly held to the highest standard as the first Person of Color to ever serve as First Lady, a role she excelled at. In spite of it, after Barack's eight-year term was up, Michelle stepped up her power and wrote her story, *Becoming*, which broke all kinds of publishing records.

I think it is important to mention Michelle's story in my book because she opened up about the trade-offs she made supporting Barack's quest for the

White House. She's relatable to any contemporary woman, but perhaps especially to accompanying spouses moving to support their partner's career.

Since my husband covered eight Presidential campaigns and the White House for *Time* magazine, and our son attended the same independent school as the Obamas, Michelle's story resonates with me in a personal way. Mostly, I just love the way she captures the quest for equality that many spouses envision achieving in marriage but which remains elusive at times, even for a First Lady.

If you are an accompanying spouse, I highly recommend you read Michelle's book and consider how she managed with her two young children, her distaste for the political spotlight and her own goals shape-shifting in support of her husband's ambitions, her girls' welfare, and the nation's ongoing needs. Since all marriages have some version of these trade-offs, Michelle's reflections are widely applicable. I admire her greatly and I look forward to learning much more from her in her middle years.

LACE-UP YOUR CHANEL BOOTS

You, dear reader, are as first-class as Jackie and Michelle. You have carried on as they have out of necessity, out of social convention, out of sheer will and determination, out of lack of another plan, out of sheer exhaustion, or even out of simple financial dependence.

As you start walking up the integration mountain in this season of moving in your middle years, you may be frightened into thinking that if you so much as touch the losses and trade-offs you've made that you will destroy the family and everything you've worked for.

You fear that you are invisible and that if you call attention to your invisibility, the last string – the family itself – will be swept up into a current and you'll lose it.

Your voice is important, and it merits healing, like Jackie's, like Michelle's, and like all human voices. But you must be willing to walk through the fear of being invisible in order to get across to the other side of your grief. That is how a mindful mover is made, and that is how you will reclaim your voice, tap into your power, and start making a difference right where you've been planted.

This is the way winter works over a fallow field, making it anew in spring.

RANT AND RECLAIM, RAVE AND REVISE

Grab a pen and paper and set a timer for thirty minutes of soul writing. Remember not to edit or judge yourself in this exercise. This is a chance to rant and reclaim, rave and revise. Follow the prompts below and let your soul speak:

- How is this move working or not working?
- Who or what do you miss most in this move?
- Expand on what you miss most. Is it a former version of yourself? Your spouse? Another love? The butcher, the baker, the candlestick maker from another life? Get specific.
- Is the loss temporary or permanent? Use your gut instinct to make a prediction.
- How are you planning to get beyond the losses of this move?
- Are you open to making friends across race, culture, and backgrounds? Why or why not?
- What are some of the other failures you've already experienced? Who can help you frame social failure in a lighthearted way?
- What is the change you wish to see in the world?
- How are you contributing to making these changes a reality?
- What's your go-to when you realize your new relationships are shallow and superficial?

- What's a simple action step to build inclusivity for you or others?
- What advice, insight, or encouragement can you offer women who have not had the advantage of moving around as much as you?

Repeat these writing prompts whenever you feel like gaining insight into your transition. By collecting them in one place, such as a journal, you'll be able to look at progress and areas where you're still ranting and raving, revising and reclaiming.

WHERE ARE YOUR DREAMS ROOTING?

I hate to bring everything back to your agency, dear reader, but that's how you'll make the integration.

Take a breath and then another. Ponder where you are at this moment in your dreams. Grief and its myriad lessons can help snap you into a long view, but only if you understand the dynamics. Plant your revised dreams anew in each location you find yourself. That way, there is continuity, and your prayers can be evolved.

And remember this tidbit of wisdom which I meant to share earlier: Your identity was never fixed; it was only your routines that were predictable. When you build back up your routines in your new place, you'll support a new sense of identity.

The world will scream at you to be stable and to be fixed, but the nature of identity is dynamic and as wiggly as gelatin. Like the ocean tides charted in tables, watch them change when a full moon, a heavy rain, or a tropical storm comes around.

Identities in flux, grief that is amorphous, and steadfastly rebuilding routines; welcome to the superpowers of relocation artistry.

WRITING YOUR RELOCATION RESUMÉ

Play is healing after a move, and sometimes it's fun to let your grief speak out in a resumé that captures all of the moves you have made in your life. Think about crafting your own Relocation Resumé and post it up on the fridge. By writing up the dates of your various moves without a lot of narrative, you will quantify the intangibles of relocation while sharpening up your sense of accomplishment. Looking over the various reinventions you have managed to perform, you'll find it hard not to be proud of the magic you've worked to date.

I provide a link to a template for the resumé in the Resources section of the book. Download a copy or take out your crayons, markers, and paints and make a big, bold Relocation Resumé for yourself when you are ready.

12

SOMEPLACE LIKE HOME

Creative expression tends to invite a certain synchronicity to the table. This morning's drafting brought Jeff the Rat Trapper. Yes, dear reader, as I was sitting down to muse on the topic of everyday nature and how she's the best relocation coach in the world, I had to chuckle because I was having an "everyday nature" moment myself.

Last week I spotted the telltale signs of California's finest up in our attic. While I do not kill spiders and I love snakes, the only rat I will let take up space in my house is my Real Authentic Transparent self. So I booked Jeff's first available appointment to set traps for me. I then forgot all about it.

He's come and gone now, and humane traps have been set. I'll call the roofer later as, apparently, the critters have chewed right through the roof. Aren't they something? Perhaps, just like you and me, all the rats are looking for is someplace like home.

While I don't recommend sheltering with rodents, I have such a deep respect for nature and her majesty that I don't need to work hard to shake off the squeamish feelings rats conjure. But how about you? Did this story make you squirm?

I have never before needed to call a rat trapper, and I would guess few of you have either. Since moving to California, in addition to phenomenal coastal life; brilliant redwood forests; phenomenal canyons; and epic deserts, lakes, and mountains, I've discovered that the state has lots of rats.

When we first arrived, I was shocked to learn how commonplace the Golden State's rodent problem was. In fact, I was sitting poolside at a fancy dinner party a couple of weeks into our move when I saw a huge rat take a straight vertical climb up an illuminated palm tree that was nearly forty-feet high. I gasped and pointed at it, but the host just nodded and said, "They love the palms," then tasted another forkful of his grilled meat.

I've adjusted now, and you too will adjust to your new home and the everyday nature surrounding you. In time, your neighborhood's flora and fauna will pattern itself into your psyche so that whatever shows up will be simple garden variety nature. In time, even if you've got a snake in the house or an exotic black furry spider to ward off, you won't feel helpless or under siege because, by then, you'll have your roster of helpers – like Jeff – vetted and at the ready, for a small fee.

OLD SOUL, NEW PLACE?

I like to believe that I am an old soul. So is every new place I have ever landed.

How do two old souls get to know one another? They check things out. It's a dance, really. The dance of settling down and finding ease is about keeping a "beginner's mind" and remaining open to what your surroundings are teaching you.

One of the Beginner's Mind feelings that is so uncomfortable to tolerate at thirty, forty, fifty – any age – is at the heart of the challenge you'll encounter in Phase III of the relocation rite of passage.

CONSCIOUS INCOMPETENCE

It happens when your soul is exhausted from managing all of the changes, and it craves a return to the feelings of ease and flow it remembers having achieved in the past. This uncomfortable feeling is called "conscious incompetence," and I use it to describe the disorientation and comparative self-judgment you are likely to experience after the boxes are unpacked and life takes on an outward appearance of being settled.

I feel consciously incompetent when:

- I am aware that I am working hard to recreate and relearn the fabric of my family's rich life
- I doubt whether relocating was wise
- I feel full of grief over all that I've given up in order to keep the family together
- I am overwhelmed and have no routine
- When so much of my daily life is spent rebuilding low-level life details instead of flying high in the creative realm where I prefer to be

According to Wikipedia, the term "conscious incompetence" comes from management trainer Martin M. Broadwell who, in 1969, used it in his "four levels of teaching" model.

Today, the model is widely applied by coaches and communicators everywhere.

I was taught the model at Duke Integrative Medicine, where I trained to become an integrated health coach in 2015. We were given the model to help us guide clients through behavior change and the adoption of a new skill. It's a useful frame, one that is widely applicative to personal development. It looks like this when adapted to adjusting to a move:

A seasoned, mindful mover quickly recognizes herself as consciously incompetent in her new home-place; she's quite aware of the fact that she's searching and rebuilding routines and patterns in hopes of restoring ease and creating someplace like home.

The less savvy mover will start the relocation journey in a worse place – perhaps in the position of unconscious incompetence – believing that moving is easy and that geographic changes are all about changes on the material plane. Sometimes in a couple, the partners will start their move at different places; one of the partners may be conscious about moving challenges while the other is not.

Unconscious incompetence about relocation can be extremely damaging because one partner may feel abandoned and left to manage through the grief all alone. Tragically, it's more common than you think, but more about that in the next chapter.

For now, what I'd like you to do is set a timer for twenty minutes so that we can do an assessment of your attachment to nature in your new place. Grab a pen and a piece of paper and, in twenty minutes, complete the following questions:

THE SOMEPLACE LIKE HOME ASSESSMENT

1. Can you point in the direction of East? How about West? North? South?
2. Look at the closest tree. What is it called? What else do you know about it?
3. Name ten local birds? Which ones have you spotted?
4. What is a highway that runs north or south near you?
5. What highway runs east or west?
6. What is your favorite street to walk? Why?
7. What is a street you prefer to avoid? Why?
8. Do you have a favorite park or hike?
9. Is there a farm stand or market nearby? What is your area known for growing?
10. How would you describe the climate you are adjusting to?
11. Describe something you love about the outdoors right where you are.
12. Describe something you were surprised to find in your new neighborhood.
13. Pick one word that captures your first impressions of your new town.

When time's up, take a look at your answers. There is no scoring of the assessment, obviously; use it to gut-check your conscious connection to your new neighborhood and its great outdoors. If none of these questions encourages you to learn more about where you live and create that someplace like home feeling sooner, perhaps this last exercise will.

THE MOON COUNT EXERCISE

Google the phrase "average life expectancy" for your gender and location. For a white woman in the U.S., that number is 78.54 years, but I'll round up to seventy-nine. Next, calculate the number of years you expect to have left. I'm fifty-four, so seventy-nine minus fifty-four equals twenty-five.

Then calculate the number of full moons you may have left in your life as follows: Twelve is the number of moons per year on average. Multiply that by the number of years you have left, in my case, twenty-five. That makes 300 full moons left for me on average. That is not many. Won't you join me in savoring the moon wherever you are? She welcomes us all home.

WHEN MOVING HURTS THE MOST

"There is a moon inside every human being. Learn to be companions with it."

— RUMI

In the last chapter, I provided an introduction to the idea of conscious incompetence and how it triggers the uncomfortable feelings I believe are the core of relocation grief. As you move through these feelings, the goal is for you to feel more "at home" in your new surroundings. The more at ease you feel, the more integrated you are likely to be, and you will also begin to relax, which is great for your body, mind, and spirit.

The goal is to return to a normal baseline routine that feels supportive to you and to your loves as swiftly as possible, but without forcing it. We can't hurry these adjustments, nor should we linger in the zone of conscious incompetence.

While you are consciously adding emotional, cognitive, and sensory adjustments to your days, no other area of your life is stopping to give you extra room. You are expected to keep up and keep it all together.

Considering that your parenting will not be put on hold, your caregiving of elders will not stop, nor will you be expected to become less of a connected and compassionate friend, sibling, spouse, or pet owner, any unexpected challenge can be enough to knock you off of your equilibrium and compound the challenge of adjusting.

LIFE HAPPENS

Relocation can feel disorienting when everything is going well; when there is a crisis, it is doubly so, and asking for the right kind of help can save months of struggle or secondary problems, like affairs, drinking, drugs, and workaholism.

Illness, aging and death, or concerns about your pet or your child's adjustment to a new school may also be devastating to you if you are newly transplanted. There is no road map or easy solution to walking through any of these challenges, but faith has always been helpful to me when navigating a variety of parenting challenges. I share this here so that you feel encouraged to open up and talk with a good friend or a coach who can meet you where you are and give you room to express yourself.

Here in the United States, as I write this book, we are in the sixth month of the global pandemic. Since Silicon Valley is a highly mobile and diverse community, I know of at least two recently relocated families who are concerned that the prolonged and restrictive social isolation orders designed to slow down the rate of transmission of the virus are profoundly impacting their adjustment. We are all being asked to make adjustments, but when one has few friends and few rituals built to sustain the prolonged stress of the pandemic, it is natural to grow dispirited.

Further, and quite tragically, Northern California was struck by a "dome of dry lightning" this week. More than 10,000 bolts of lightning moved in from the Pacific into and up the Bay Area in the course of one day. With it came thunder and a few raindrops, but not much; this storm was nothing like the sound, fury, and drenching rains of an East Coast thunderstorm, a nor'easter, or the hurricanes I remember.

A STRANGER TO THE WEATHER

It is difficult to explain the anxiety and existential overwhelm that can be delivered like a body blow when a newly relocated person encounters a foreign weather system. All kinds of feelings can show up, including extreme fear and then, in the next breath, regret or doubt about moving in the first place. This is natural and part of the chaotic fight or flight response that is primal within us all.

Coping with new kinds of weather takes practice, and with climate change advancing, the tragic irony is that many of us will be coping with new kinds of weather even as we stay in place.

I had never witnessed nor imagined anything like Northern California's lightening complex storm. It came on the heels of extensive power outages and statewide heat records (including a 130-degree reading in Death Valley, in Southern California). The flashes of light were so strong and continuous that I couldn't help but wait in dread for what would happen next.

Would one of our gorgeous oaks be struck down? Would a neighbor's home be struck? Would there be wind and rain? There seemed to be no evidence of any immediate crisis here in the Valley until the sun came up the next day when we learned about the hundreds of fires that had been sparked overnight.

UPS AND DOWNS AND THOSE BROWN
HILLS

Remember those brown hills I mentioned walking up and down in Chapter 4? Many of them are burning right now as I write about how relocating often demands that we adjust to foreign weather patterns that shock our systems.

The largest fire burning is located to the east of the San Jose city limits. Toward the coast, there is another major fire burning a complex of 2,000-year-old redwoods in Big Basin State Park, California's oldest state park, a national treasure to all tree people.

Bay Area air quality is listed as "worst in the world" right now, and even the daily walks I was taking to deal with the pandemic are impossible. Hundreds of thousands of people, and in some cases their livestock, have been evacuated, and others have lost homes and structures. Since hundreds of inmates trained to fight wildfires were released to spare their lives from the pandemic, the state is now hustling to train additional personnel to respond to ongoing fire threats.

It would be an understatement to say that this year has been a lot for this state I now call home. While I am eternally grateful to first responders and the officials working twenty-four-seven to lower the risk of wildfire here as the climate changes, I fear that only a global cultural shift can make the impact we need to slow the course of temperatures rising.

When I shake my head and think, what am I doing here in the midst of these unprecedented fires, I remember that I asked myself a similar question when I moved with Brooks and the children from Boston into our home inside the Beltway six months after 9/11.

The question, "What am I doing here?" always reminds me to wake up to the present moment because whether one is here or there, in this place or that, every day is unprecedented.

Every place is impacted by climate change and as the weather shifts, the veil lifts. We will all discover that there is much more to learn from Earth in the decades to come, so begin the inquiry today.

Mother's fierce nature will have us as she likes us.

I say, let us make our way humbly and accept responsibility for some of the challenges we face, wherever we are. Make a commitment to yourself to learn how to be prepared in the event of local weather events, then make a small offering to heal the planet and restore the virtuous cycle of life we depend on.

For me, today was the day I got my new urban compost-maker going with scraps from a CSA delivery. I realize I am not heroically saving the planet with my composting hobby, but it did give me a centering task to tend to the Earth as she burned all around me. The women, the children, and the trees need us each to be in relationship with Earth in new ways.

BE THE OCEAN

I wish we could set a timer and say time's up to relocation adjusting (and climate change) after a season of dedicated focus, but that is magical thinking. Ongoing, enlightened steps and realignment in the face of change is the path; either the weather will challenge you, or you'll encounter other changes that will be traumatizing.

Still, I trust that you'll get through the ups and downs as best you can, hopefully by opening your heart. My experience has taught me to expect the feelings to come and go and to yield with each unexpected loss; as the Sufic teaching coaxes, "An ocean refuses no river, no river."

Another way to pass the expanse of time your adjustment will require is to make a deliberate choice to celebrate milestones in your new place. Right now, as I await the chance to gather new friends and neighbors around our very long table, the one I designed to be the center of our downsized home in our close-knit, walkable neighborhood, I feel impatient to open the doors to new friends.

We had just barely had the paint on our house

dry when the global pandemic locked our college-age kids and us down. We're still on lockdown, but the silver lining is that we are safe and that we have made a bunch of memories in our new house.

How has your move been impacted by unexpected events locally? Nationally? Globally? What are the ways those unexpected changes have accelerated or slowed your adjustment? What are you looking forward to doing to mark the milestones along your adjustment?

PLANNING FOR THE UNEXPECTED

As empty-nesters in a new town, we looked forward to downsizing and living in a walkable neighborhood that was home to mixed ages and backgrounds in America's tenth largest city. While I could envision causes I cared about, I did not anticipate being disrupted by so many unplanned impacts in my third year of adjusting after relocation. The unexpected has me revising my goals and expectations and paying attention to shifts. Perhaps that is relatable to you?

While I dreamed about making art and love and growing healthy food, I didn't foreground the global pandemic, the hormonal changes, the death of my father and the grief that followed, the bittersweet emptiness that came with launching children to college, and the aging of East Coast elders I could no longer visit regularly due to geography and then lockdown.

I mention these shocks because they are to be expected with relocation, plain and simple. But that doesn't mean you'll know how to cope with them.

While some moments call for muscling on through, other more compound traumas will call you into new kinds of inner work and release, whether you are married or not. In my case, prior to my recent relocation, my marriage had sustained multiple moves and near-constant agitation as we hustled to thrive in the cutthroat industry of photo-journalism while raising kids inside the Beltway in D.C. My particular relocation stressors present as trust issues, abandonment issues, and a great deal of frustration about the distribution of labor dynamic at work in my marriage.

You will have different struggles, surely. Perhaps you will battle unbearable homesickness in a big city, even as your life on the outside takes an exciting, cosmopolitan appearance. Perhaps you will battle unexpected levels of racism or anti-Semitism in your new small town. Or, more subtly, but deeply challenging, perhaps you will find yourself feeling unstimulated and depressed after moving out of an urban environment into a cul-de-sac of social convention in suburbia; the grief of missing the variety you once enjoyed just steps from your apartment can compound one's adjustment to a new place in complex ways.

Unpacking the story of your moves is an ongoing process that will not end. If you have moved often, then adjusting to your new home will bring more complexity into your personal narrative. This is all to be expected, so take your time and be patient as things fall into place.

MARRIAGE CHANGES TOO

In the last chapter, I set up an example of how an accompanying spouse can grow frustrated and resentful when she carries the bulk of the emotional work relocating demands. That was me, and I am still working through how it hurt and how I can continue to do better.

In my opinion, the biggest challenge for couples after moving is establishing a common narrative that they believe supports them in their adjustment to a new home, a new city, or a new town. When the children are young or the relationship is just starting out there may be a great deal of common ground about the shared narrative. After many moves the goals can become less straightforward, so the couple must become more mindful and work together to acknowledge how the move has changed them.

If one partner takes the sunny side – that the great job or the salary increases was worth the move, for instance – then the other partner may get stuck over-functioning on the shadow side, managing the grunt work of invisible but essential details that carry no social status. In that case, the shadowed partner likely won't feel that moving was worth it quite as quickly.

Similarly, if one partner ends up traveling constantly after the move, then the other partner may get stuck inside the shell of the marriage structure while desperately trying to recreate the family's new social center, alone. She or he will be starving for affection, recognition, and adult company, especially if her life is focused on re-centering the children, pets or a spouse in a new home.

While many accompanying spouses work outside of the home and re-establish careers, the division of labor at home can slow that transition. Further, the elusive boost in confidence that working outside the home promises may remain out of reach to the accompanying spouse through no fault of her own.

If one partner remains in unconscious incompetent mode while the other is consciously aware of just how difficult relocation can be, the two are likely to experience a complete disconnect. They are likely to have different narrative realities about relocation. If left unattended, this will likely be the end of their marriage, if not legally, then emotionally.

In this way, the marriage will become an empty shell as the couple defaults to staying together, either for the children, for the convenience, or simply because the idea of moving again is entirely unpalatable since they've been broken by prior moves already. It will be sad to see their love for one another become sexless under the strain of the stuffed emotions, and without intervention, the temporary separation in place will become permanent.

By then, the invisible partner may have developed a flair for the outrageous under the strain of feeling so invisible. The emotional affairs she maintains will cease bridging the gaps of her marriage, and she'll eventually give up on her dreams, especially her inner dreams of playing big and of living with her soul mate and creating a wonderful life together while making art and an impact.

Living with someone who is unconsciously incompetent and lacks self-awareness is hard to make progress with. Living with someone who is overly conscious about losses and is craving evidence of her existence from a partner is also unbearable. The only solution is for the couple to share and rebalance and see what life the partnership has left in it.

It is common to get stuck on one side of the spectrum of change for a time. Commit to doing the reflective work of adjusting to your relocation and continue to become more mindful about moving. By working through the blocks, you will become a relocation artist who contributes to a healing conversation wherever she lands in this mobile world.

INVITING GUIDANCE AND SUPPORT

If you are stuck adjusting to your move, it is important to stay open and to invite help from professionals. Relocation depressions are common. Start asking around for good groups or couples' therapists that work as relocation coaches. Don't worry if it takes a few tries to find the right chemistry.

If your partner happens to be the sole breadwinner, he or she may feel like they are in an authority position over the spending. I feel strongly that asking for and paying for help is one investment the two of you can't afford to not make. Resentments only grow stronger when emotional connectivity is repeatedly denied. One partner's blocked grief will become the other partner's bag of rocks to carry. It's not worth it.

These scenarios are not uncommon, and if your marriage is hurting, there is no reason to be ashamed. The joy awaits you on the other side, but without assistance, the asymmetry between you and your spouse will infect the entire relationship until – on top of relocation trauma – you'll have other things to manage in your middle years.

Sadly, I have found that many therapists and life coaches are not aware of the extent of the challenge relocators face, and there is a lot of gender bias that accompanying spouses who are women must maneuver in therapy in order to be heard and empowered. Therapists will focus on outer issues and language, but they do not generally come with an appreciation for relocation as a rite of passage from the inside out. These nuances are vital to healing and supporting someone who is working to achieve that at home feeling.

While both members of the couple should be encouraged to keep a differentiated point of view, they may need help creating a unified, equitable framework that yokes them together like oxen plowing a field. It will be hard work to manage the farm of a marriage on the move, and I consider it cruel to leave the inner work of moving solely on the shoulders of the more domestic partner.

Further, the idea of reciprocity beyond transactional aspects of marriage is a challenge for some partners to comprehend and to incorporate in their relationship. In these cases, as the experience of loneliness and isolation show up, and one partner is unable or unwilling to acknowledge the nature of the painful feelings, a chilling asymmetry enters the narrative.

WISE ACTION, COMPASSIONATE PARTNERSHIP

If an accompanying spouse's unattended needs are not met with compassion and action, and he or she does not get support to make the adjustment, they are at risk of unknowingly destroying the marriage, their social status, and, quite possibly the spouse's career, too.

In fact, I have read that the number one reason assignments abroad fail is due to the emotional issues families struggle with after relocation. I would guess that it is common with stateside relocations as well.

That is why it is so important to become more mindful of the extent to which unconsciousness slows down relocation adjustments. That is what this entire book is about.

Putting language on issues that matter without blaming and judgment is the path to making friends and enjoying life. You are moving toward a flow in order to feel at-home faster – wherever life takes you.

CONCLUSION

You made the move, and you are on your way to creating someplace like home.

As you adjust to millions of new inputs, some of them anticipated, others unexpected, you'll feel highs and lows and everything in between. While you continue to cycle through the changes, remember all the ways moving is a rite of passage. Recapping:

- Separation is the foundation to a great move, but it is also the most likely to be shortchanged in the rush to get all the moving details done;
- Transition is the shortest part of a relocation artist's passage, but one that is highly demanding of time, money, and energy;

- Integration and incorporation is the life-changing, long, often diffuse phase of a relocation and one that provides you lots of opportunity for reflection about trade-offs, relative wins and losses, and grief.

I hope you'll practice some of the techniques outlined in the book, and if you follow just one tip, it is to look for clues in everyday nature to help you unpack your soul first and feel at home sooner.

THE MOVER'S MINDSET

One of the most exciting things about moving a lot is looking back and admiring the mover's mindset you've earned for yourself. With your tuned-up mover's mindset, I bet you start seeing yourself as a powerhouse, not simply as a trailing spouse or a moving mouse, timid and hiding from life. Step into your power and place, and see what kind of difference you can make right where you've landed.

Relocation artists welcome change and variety. They balance grounded life in a specific community, but they are likely to be a bit less attached to material possessions and common measures of social status. They are divergent thinkers and have seen a lot. They are likely to be creative too.

From my perspective, the relocation artist is one of the most interesting creative people one can become, and the experience is likely to provide a person with an empathetic lens through which to observe the world and its unfolding.

A relocation artist is generally understated. She is also painfully aware of the need for community and friendship as a life force. She is private and walks the Earth humbly.

You'll see her regularly and fluidly cross traditional lines of culture, race, and socio-economic demographics as she creates someplace like home for herself, what she loves, and anyone she invites into her circle.

In fact, I bet there are dozens of relocation artists quietly at work in your new community. You will be better at spotting them now that you are initiated. Even if she looks different, speaks a different language, wears different clothing, and follows different customs, if she helps you feel at home sooner, then I guarantee she's a relocation artist, just like you.

CO-CREATING THE CHANGE

When you feel frustrated and full of self-doubt, remember to recall the gardener's ditty:

First year it sleeps, second year it creeps, third year it leaps.

That is you, and by now, you are starting to leap.

It is likely that it will take at least well into your third year before you and your beautiful new soul garden leap. Stay steady and remain patient before you make any judgments about the merits of your move. If you need help to avoid getting stuck, reach out for some coaching, or find a great therapist in your town.

As you root into life in your new place, the world will continue to work on you. Keep making memories, keep counting moons, and consider how you, right where you are, can start co-creating the better places on earth with all of the experience you have. We need your wisdom.

JUST ONE WILD AND PRECIOUS LIFE

Habitat is powerful, and as climate change disrupts all of our plans for living, why wouldn't we, at times, feel like the lone polar bear floating far from shore on a stray piece of Arctic ice, separated from the mainland unexpectedly? Whether you are moving or not, consider the search for stable habitat a universal and urgent need.

As the fires of our lives burn existentially and the Arctic ice melts at a record pace, as we relocate for love, for money, or for spiritual seeking, the Earth's subtle and not so subtle energies will continue speaking to us, upending so-called regular life and its trappings.

At times we will be stranded, whether alone or in our marriage, in our hometowns or abroad, able bodied or not, with or without work at times. There is no straight line, just steps at a time. Be where you are and who you are while there too.

Be considerate of yourself and others when you are stuck and stranded because there is no plan, just steps at a time.

The invitation calling out like birdsong to each and every one of us at different seasons of our lives is here and growing louder. Can you hear it too? Consider how you want to use the many dimensions of in-between space you are experiencing after your move to craft, as the Jungians would say, a life of greater authenticity and meaning.

Trust that when you start the journey inward, you will see it never stops. Moving introduces you to infinity in bittersweet cycles, and these will awaken you to the finite aspects of your humble human life. It's a paradox. Our smallness expands us and sets us free to live fully and in the present.

As poet Mary Oliver says best in her poem "The Summer Day:"

Tell me, what is it you plan to do with your one wild and precious life?

AFTERWORD

Twenty-seven years ago, I had a plane ticket to Russia and a grant that would allow me to stay there for two years. As the day for departure drew near, my sense of adventure and confidence dwindled. *Why am I choosing to fly across the world – to Siberia no less – where I know not a soul and have no experience doing this work?* I asked myself. I was full of self-criticism for pursuing what had been my long-held dream to build connections between US and Russian conservation scientists through this two-year project. My dream come true suddenly seemed like a really dumb idea.

Aware of my growing doubts, Christine Kraft, one of my closest friends from college, arrived at my childhood home in rural Massachusetts with a tote bag of books, pads of paper and pens. We had graduated three years earlier and she was living and working in Boston. As a "head resident" of our dormitory in college, Christine had honed her natural-born talents as a listener, empath, and advisor to smart young women. Now she was at my kitchen table, friend and coach, to help launch me on my way. For the next three hours, we spread out her materials, drawing flow charts and graphs, and mapping out a plan for my future work in the remote reaches of Russia. Our kitchen planning session became the first of many coaching conversations which have continued into my career in Arctic wildlife conservation for a leading international environmental organization.

Over the last three decades, as educational film maker, pioneer in documenting individuals' personal health care narratives, artist, life coach, and director of a non-profit organization, Christine has continued to develop her innate skills in clear seeing and empathy for all beings. Through Duke Integrative Medicine's Professional Health Coaching program, she gained additional training and built a network of colleagues in her field. But it is Christine's own life experience as someone who has moved around the country and tapped into clairvoyant-like intuition which make her a remarkable sounding board and teacher.

As a client of Aphrodite Works, I've experienced Christine's unique approach: a mix of humor, an understanding of human (especially feminine) nature, and razor-sharp vision. In her book, you've spotted her approach as she shares the intimate and sometimes painful experience of learning to be an "accompanying spouse" and mother who is also a professional with her own aspirations and brilliant ideas. Weaving in strands of Buddhism and Sufism, along with philosophy and poetry, comes naturally for Christine.

Christine cautions that relocation is not just about ticking off checklists, taping boxes, waving goodbye to neighbors, and rushing on to set up the furniture in a new house. Rather, she tells us, reflection, self-care, and willingness to welcome the intense emotions around moving are essential steps toward creating ease, even peace, in the process.

As a person who regularly seeks nature as a refuge, I am compelled by Christine's own connection with the natural world and call to fully engage in one's surroundings as a critical step in the moving transition, or any transition at all. Noticing the insect life, tuning into local birdsong, tasting the water, orienting to the area's landscape helps to ground us, quite literally. This is not to say that the transition is easy, or results will be instantaneous. Neither polar bears nor plants can be plopped down hundreds of miles from their natural range and be expected to adapt quickly; why should humans be any different?

In the end, however, there is no "right" way to move, nor a right way to transition. This basic truth and many other lessons in the book apply to nearly all aspects of life, making it relevant even to non-movers. As she reminds us: "There is no such thing as picking the best path; that's a fictitious route. It's about picking a path, period." Finally, *Unpacked* is a call for mindful, deliberative living. In considering how many full moons await us in our remaining years, Christine invites us: "won't you join me in savoring the moon wherever you are? She welcomes us all home."

Margaret Williams, Environmentalist, Anchorage, AK

October 2020

RESOURCES

- **Make Your Own Soil Rubbing**: aphroditeworks.com/blog/soil-rubbing
- **Create a Relocation Resume**: aphroditeworks.com/blog/relocation-resume
- **Take the Someplace Like Home Assessment**: aphroditeworks.com/blog/someplace-like-home-assessment

ACKNOWLEDGMENTS

For my mother, who loved the garden, and my mother-in-law, who made moving look easy. With thanks to my father and to my father-in-law, as well as to all of my talented aunties and uncles; I carry the foundation of family you provided.

To my Long Island loves – the formative creatives of my East End childhood, Kim, Kay, Alex, Dawn, Bud, Amanda, James et Jean, T.R., Hammy, Gayle and Peter.

To my Smith College, Boston University, and Cambridge/Boston crew, especially: Claudia and Jamie, Eliza, Susan, Genie, Tonya and Orhun, Jane, Doreen, Jim and Trish, Annette, Jon and Ellen, and to all of my teachers, especially Don, Paul and Jonathan.

With love to my Washington, D.C., crew, whose sophistication and warmth stays first in class, right with our kids. Thank you for the friendship and teaching: Denielle, Beth, Bettina, Maria, Louise, Lisa, Laura, Karen, Alison, Tisha, Gina, Carol, Smitha, Jacquie, Anne, Jacki, Suzanne, Kathleen, Dahlia, Carrington, Sally, Lisa, Amy, Marjan, Estee, Dianne, Nicole, Danna, Nell, Sherry, Julia, Tessa, Margaret, friends from the SFS Quaker Life and MLK committees, DCVLP friends, Heather and the Revolution Health gang, and to all the Health 2.0 and Walking Gallery collaborators, real and virtual over the years, especially Regina, Ted, Susannah, Dave, Alex, John, Charles and Gautam. To Duke Integrative Medicine friends and colleagues helping create change, a person at a time, especially to Dave, Sherri, Kim, and friends from Cohort 23.

With love to my new tribe in the Bay Area: Carole, Renee, Michele, Christina, Marianne, Eva, Lisa, Lori, Kathryn, K. T. and Mike, Dana and Yori, Leena, Janis, Lynda, Clorinda, Mary Lou, Tiphani, Gerry and Heather, Harry, Pam, the Visual Philosophy artists, my Powerhouse sisters, Chandra, Mo, Erika, Elizabeth, Annette, Marla and Miriam, and new friends, age 30 to 103, at the San Jose Woman's Club.

Thanks to Hans Wydler, in D.C., and to Paul Younan, in Los Gatos, CA for the expert real estate guidance and support they provided to us.

With thanks to Dan Haar for brainstorming early on in the writing process, and to Cory Hott and

Madeline Kosten for editorial magic and Elena Burnett for proofreading wizardry.

To Penney Peirce, an expansive thank you for the wisdom, the mentoring and the bright light you shine in the Foreword.

To Margaret Williams, a "moonful" of gratitude for the afterword you wrote and for supporting the Aphrodite Works vision from day one.

To my sisters Deirdre, Elizabeth, and Theresa for their trifecta of healing power across many moves and many moons, and to my brothers Richard, Steve, and Victor for the laughter.

Finally, to my love and mad moving companion, Brooks, and our beautiful children, Ella and Daniel. Thank you for 28 years of adventure and for all the help unpacking our story.

ABOUT THE AUTHOR

Christine Kraft is a storyteller, artist and coach. Daughter of a therapist and a computer entrepreneur, she grew up exploring the beautiful Atlantic shores of Long Island's East End. It was there she started mapping wetlands, sunrises, butterflies, and bogs. It was there she started dreaming of a big, bold, beautiful life of service and deep friendship.

Christine has been fascinated by people and their stories since birth. A curious soul, she studied Medical Anthropology at Smith College, then went on to earn a Master of Science at Boston University's College of Communication. She spent two decades carving out a niche for herself in health technology, contributing to more than 100 personal stories designed to give patients, providers, and caregivers a voice.

Today, from her home in the heart of Silicon Valley, Christine is in the third year of her relocation from the East Coast. She supports a variety of social and environmental causes and is the founder of Aphrodite Works, an intuitive mentoring practice that combines creative expression, language, personal storytelling, and coaching.

She is Mindfulness Based Stress Reduction (MBSR) certified and also holds a certificate from Duke Integrative Medicine Health Coaching. She looks forward to spending her middle years working with clients in the art studio, in nature, at the office, and in the kitchen.

Unpacked is her first book.

Healing the Healer Within: 8 Steps to Unleash Your Potential by Dr. Cheri McDonald

Ocean of Possibilities: Maximize Natural Cancer Healing with Marine Organisms and Functional Medicine by Heather Moretzsohn

Will I Ever Get Pregnant?: The Smart Woman's Guide to Get Pregnant Naturally Over 40 by Tsao-Lin E. Moy

The Successful Canna-preneur: The Practical Guide to Thrive in the Legal Cannabis Space by JM Balbuena

The Evolving Home: The Conscious Design Guide to Restoring Function and Comfort in the New Normal by Kadie Remaklus

Voices of Fibro: The Guidebook for Moms Seeking to Care and Support Their Child Living with Fibromyalgia by Mildred Velez

Ultimate Fulfillment: A Blueprint for Finding and Living Your Purpose by Dr. Joy Kwakuyi

THANK YOU

Thank you for reading. If you are a relocation artist, you've crossed lots of borders.

I'd like to invite you to check out the Border Women Project at Aphrodite Works, http://www. aphroditeworks.com/the-border-women.

I try to offer a free download or poster as often as I am able to. Look for the link.

Made in the USA
Columbia, SC
28 October 2020

23587500R00095